I think you've done it, my friend! You said you wanted to write something that would deliver hope to those faced with enormous heartache. You've shown us where hope is found—in a loving Heavenly Father!

Your sister in struggles,

Gracia Burnham
Author of *In the Presence of My Enemies*
and *To Fly Again*

Lynnette's story is tender and provides practical hope for those in the journey of suffering through the loss of a baby or child and for those facing uncertainty and fear when a child faces a medical crisis. Her transparent sharing, practical insights, and purpose-filled pain will encourage you to embrace God's timeless truth and love to carry you through your pain and grief.

Kathe Wunnenberg
Author of *Grieving The Child I Never Knew, Grieving the Loss of a Loved One, Longing for a Child*

In Faithfulness,

He Afflicted Me

In Faithfulness,
He
Afflicted
Me

*A mother finds
purpose and victory
through heartache.*

Lynnette Kraft

TATE PUBLISHING *& Enterprises*

Published by Tate Publishing & Enterprises, LLC
127 E. Trade Center Terrace | Mustang, Oklahoma 73064 USA
1.888.361.9473 | www.tatepublishing.com

Tate Publishing is committed to excellence in the publishing industry. The company reflects the philosophy established by the founders, based on Psalm 68:11,
"The Lord gave the word and great was the company of those who published it."

Book design copyright © 2008 by Tate Publishing, LLC. All rights reserved.
Cover design by Stefanie Rooney
Interior design by Lance Waldrop
Cover Photo by Kelsy Gossett

Published in the United States of America

ISBN: 978-1-60604-952-5
1. Christian Living: Practical Life: Grief, Suffering, Consolation
2. Christian Living: Relationships: Family Concerns
08.07.07

Dedication

My dear Kyle. I would like to dedicate this book to you. God definitely had a plan when he paired us up! We've had some wonderful times, and we've shared deep sorrow. I'm grateful that we've done it all side by side. Having you in my life has made me blossom into who God always wanted me to be. I never would have had the confidence to write this book without you cheering me on. I love you, Dearest, and I thank you for loving me so sincerely.

My precious children—Jared, Samuel, Abigail, Josiah, Cecily, Anna, Silas, Jonas, and Harrison—I would also like to dedicate this book to you. Your lives made my story what it is. God has used each and every one of you in my life in a very special way. For those of you who have gone on to heaven before me, your lives touched me in a way that will never be forgotten. I miss you, but I know I'll see you again! For those of you who are still with me, I love being your momma, and I'm so glad we are such good friends. I know that the Lord has a bright future for you all. Some of you have experienced heartache with me, but you've depended on the Lord, as I have, and we are all better for it somehow. I love you all with my whole heart.

Contents

Introduction

Can I truly say without reservation that I'm grateful for my trials and the burdens that I've been called to bear? Has God's hand been evident enough that I can be sure he has worked through the heartaches that he has allowed in my life? The answer is a resounding *yes!*

It is amazing, marvelous, and at times miraculous what God has done to show me that he cares, that he is near, and that his plans are not to harm me but to prosper me and give me a future and a hope.

The wisdom and insight I have gained have not only been a true revelation of the love of God and his tender care and protection, but I have also gained a new perspective. God chose a path for me that I never would have chosen for myself, but having traveled it, I can truly say I'm grateful for my journey.

Prologue

I awoke suddenly to hear my six-year-old daughter Anna loudly crying out. I glanced at the clock. It was 3:23 a.m. I threw the covers off of myself, quickly got out of bed, and hurried to her room. I was surprised to see Cecily still asleep next to her and little brother Silas still sleeping in his toddler bed next to theirs.

"What's wrong, Anna?" I asked with a frantic heart. Anxiously she said, "I don't feel well, and I *do not* know why." I wondered if she had a migraine. They were not uncommon for Anna. I'd always wondered if her lower oxygen level was a reason that she got them. "Do you have a headache?" I asked.

"No, it's not a headache. I don't know what it is, but I feel really sick." I picked her up and hurried her to the bathroom. She immediately threw up. It wasn't like other times when she'd thrown up; it was very violent and loud. It surprised me and scared me. Her heart began to beat so fast and hard, I could see her chest moving with each beat.

"Are you okay, sweetie?" I asked while gently rubbing my hands against her arms and giving her a sympathetic look.

"Yes, I feel a little better. Mommy, may I please take a bath?" While Anna was in the bath, we prayed. We prayed that she would feel better and that God would take away her pain. I then sat and talked to her. It was November and Christmas was right around the corner. To get her mind off of being sick, I began to talk about Christmas presents.

"What would you like for Christmas?" Was my question to distract her.

"A little brown box to put my treasures in, like Lydia's," she said. Lydia was one of Anna's special friends that she had just spent some time with that week. She also told me that she would like a newborn baby doll and a pretty dress. I'm not sure the distraction was working that well, but she was playing along. She wanted me to think she was feeling better, but the look in her eyes and her pale face spoke volumes.

I got her out of the tub and she threw up again. For the moment she was feeling a little better, so I got her dressed, took her to her room, and crawled into bed with her. Her heart was beating fast, which caused her breathing to be labored. I could tell that she wasn't comfortable. I began to panic a little. She had had a couple of similar episodes in the past, but both of those times it lasted for a short time and then she was fine. I tried to talk myself out of worrying.

I propped myself up on some pillows and laid Anna in front of me; her back was to my tummy. She could breathe better when she wasn't flat on her back. I could feel her heart beating against me. I stroked her wavy brown hair and rubbed her soft little cheeks and her forehead. I was anxious, but I tried to breathe very slow and steady. With

Anna lying against me, I thought that my own breathing pattern might affect hers.

I silently talked to God about Anna and asked him to calm my fears and make her better. I reminded him how special she was to me and how hard it was to watch her suffer. I hoped that she would relax in my arms and that her heart would slow down. It did a little.

After a few minutes she said, "I feel *so* much better now." Ah, what a relief to hear those words! I can deal with my own pain and suffering, but to have to watch my children suffer is a great burden to bear. I can't think of much that is more difficult for me.

I assumed she had the stomach flu and that the vomiting was what made her heart race, but I decided at that moment that I would call her cardiologist first thing in the morning. Somewhere deep down I wondered if there was more to it, but I wasn't prepared to go there with my thoughts. If it was her heart, the next step would probably be a heart and lung transplant. I was frightened by those thoughts.

We had enjoyed over six years with Anna, and most of those years were fairly uneventful as far as her heart was concerned. Recently things had changed in her health, but even her doctor didn't see a big change in her heart function when he had given her a thorough examination. Maybe only I noticed, but she just hadn't been herself.

After spending about fifteen minutes with Anna lying against me, Jonas, our one-year-old, woke up to nurse. He was in my bedroom, so I told Anna I would be right back. I propped her up against a few pillows and went into my bedroom. Kyle was just waking up to get ready for work, so I asked, "Honey, can you please get Anna and bring her in here? She isn't feeling well."

He went and picked her up and said, "You're not feeling well, huh?" She just shook her head and cuddled up against her Daddy's chest. He laid her in his spot on our bed, pulled the covers up over her, gave her a kiss, and went to the bathroom across the hall to get ready for work.

I had nursed Jonas for about ten minutes when Anna sat up very suddenly and screamed. It sounded like fear more than anything, but I could immediately tell she was sick. I quickly put Jonas on the bed. Thank goodness I had given him enough to satisfy him. He was awake but didn't fuss when I put him down.

I grabbed a cup that was on the nightstand and put it in front of Anna's mouth. She threw up. She continued to cry out with severe intensity. I immediately panicked. I frantically said, "Anna, you're going to hurt yourself!" I was not only afraid of what was causing her pain and fear, but I was certain that her weak heart couldn't handle this degree of intensity for long. She then threw her head back and fell onto the bed. I tried to set her up. I was afraid she would throw up and choke on it. She wouldn't get up. In fact, I couldn't even force her up—her body was arched back and stiff.

I began to scream for Kyle…nothing…I screamed again…he still couldn't hear me! I hurried off of the bed, flipped on the light, and screamed for Kyle from the doorway. He finally heard me and came running in with fear in his eyes.

"Call 911! Hurry! Something is wrong with Anna!" I said with extreme panic in my voice.

Somehow, he remembered that the phone was in Jared's room. Of course Jared, Anna's 14-year-old brother, woke up. He ran in and saw his little sister. She looked very abnormal and was making strange noises. Kyle told him to take Jonas and go to his bedroom to pray. He quickly obeyed.

When we realized that her heart wasn't beating, Kyle and I began to do CPR. The phone call had been made. Kyle was on the phone yelling, "Hurry up…oh, Anna, honey, please hang on. You can't die, Anna. Hang on for us!" Crying, he pleaded, "Please hurry! Are you almost here? She's not breathing!" Kyle was frantic. It was all so sudden. He didn't go to bed worried like I did, and he hadn't been up with her.

We had never done CPR on a real person before, but we had taken classes when Anna was a baby. They wouldn't let us leave the hospital with her until we had learned how to perform the procedure. I had hoped we'd never have to use those skills.

I was very quiet. I wouldn't say I was calm, because I didn't feel that way. What would be the outcome of this nightmare? From the moment it all began, I had wondered if it was Anna's time to enter heaven. I guess it could have been God giving me a resolve in my spirit, but I didn't trust my feelings, and in fact, rejected them.

I was nervous and somewhat frantic in my thoughts, yet there was a strange peace as well.

It's kind of hard to describe all that was going through my mind. Kyle was doing chest compressions, and I was attempting to breathe life into my little girl. I did it without saying a word, but my whole body trembled. It was difficult to perform this necessary task, because I was breathing like any person who was in shock and panicked. My breaths were quick and shallow.

Kyle cried and begged the man on the phone to get somebody to our house and pleaded with God and with Anna. He was desperate. I felt every emotion he was feeling, but I let him verbalize it. I remained quiet.

After doing CPR for what seemed like an eternity, Anna's heart began to beat very slowly. Her eyes that had been looking towards us began to look the other direction as though she was looking at something else. Perhaps there was something much more precious to see on her other side. I began to sing to her, "Jesus loves me this I know. For the Bible tells me so. Little ones to him belong. They are weak but he is strong." I said, "Anna, Jesus is right here with you. Don't be afraid. He will take care of you, honey. I love you, I love you, I love you." Her heart quit beating.

We frantically began CPR again. We knew in our hearts she was gone, but when you love somebody that much, that reality is very hard to face. We were going to fight with everything we had to keep her with us. Kyle and I kept saying to each other, between breaths, that we thought she was gone. It was as though we wanted to make sure that the other was prepared to accept what both of us knew had just happened.

We finally heard sirens. Jared ran to let them in. A man ran up the stairs and began CPR right away. When Anna didn't respond, he immediately picked her up, threw her over his shoulder and ran down the stairs. Maybe he was trained to handle a situation like this in this way, but I would have felt better if he would have carried her in his arms. Watching Anna dangle over his shoulder like that was heart-wrenching.

He took her to the ambulance, laid her on the gurney, cut and tore her Winnie the Pooh shirt to expose her chest, and then the paramedics began to work on her. They worked quickly. We knew we were heading to the hospital. I had my pajamas on, but Kyle had to run in and get some clothes on. I jumped in the ambulance, but they told me I couldn't be in there. I was still in shock. I felt like I was walking around in a daze. Everything happening was very surreal. I just felt a strange confusion and numbness.

Kyle and I followed the ambulance in our car. We wondered what was happening to our daughter. She had been without breath and a heartbeat so long; was it even possible after all this time to get her back. We really felt that she was with Jesus, but how can you give up hope until somebody tells you to. Jared asked before we left if she was going to be okay. We told Jared that we thought she was already with the Lord. We didn't want him to think she was suffering. I hated to leave him at home after what he had just experienced, but somebody had to stay with the other children.

On the way to the hospital we weren't crying, at least I don't remember crying. I think I felt that if I didn't cry, I was being more hopeful. Maybe she would be okay if I assumed she would be, but in my heart I think I knew that she was already gone.

We called my parents, who lived thirty-five minutes away, and asked them to go and be with Jared and the other children. I called my friend Renee and told her I thought Anna was with Jesus. Renee's reaction really affected me. She wasn't asleep like the others had been when we called. She immediately understood. She wept severely. Her daughter Laura was frantically asking her what was wrong. She told her that Anna had died.

When she said that, it hit me like a ton of bricks. My sweet little daughter was gone. I would not hear her voice, or see her sweet little smiling face, or cuddle her warm soft body again, until we were together again in heaven. Oh, I hoped that it wouldn't be long. I begged the Lord to come and get us all at that moment. I didn't want to live anymore. The pain was unbearable, but I resisted it. I knew she was gone, but I was still hoping for a miracle, trying to convince myself that my feelings were wrong.

When we got to the hospital, I was told to go to the desk and give them information. The lady behind the counter started asking me questions. She wanted Anna's name, our address, and other information. I couldn't remember anything. I cried and became confused. Every part of my body was shaking. She didn't say, "I'm sorry." She just looked at me like, *Come on lady, just tell me what I need to know, and then you can get back to your daughter.* When I was done giving her the information that she needed, I went back to Kyle and Anna.

Anna still wasn't breathing, and her heart was still not beating. It had been nearly forty-five minutes since the nightmare began. We knew there was no way she was coming back to us, and we didn't want those people touching her anymore. I was grateful for their efforts, but at the time, all I could think was, *These people don't know what a precious little girl this is, they don't know how close we are or how much we love her.* We wanted our daughter to ourselves. We wanted those strangers to leave her alone.

Kyle told them that if they didn't think she was going to come back to us, we wanted a chance to say goodbye. It was strange how we were treated. I felt like they thought we hurt Anna. The staff just kind of wandered away.

We went to our precious daughter. Daddy kissed her for each of our children. He said, "This one's for Jared, this one's for Abigail, this one's for Cecily, this one's for Silas, this one's for Jonas." We both told her how special she was to us and that we looked forward to the day we would see her again.

A while later some hospital workers came back in and removed the needles and tubes and bags and everything else they had attached to her, and we began to stroke her and touch her and kiss her and talk to her. In a way I hoped that she was watching us say goodbye, but at the same time, I didn't want her to see us crying. I didn't want her to see her mommy and daddy with such intense sorrow. I didn't want her to be sad. I wanted her to rejoice that she was in the presence of our almighty God! I didn't want her to look back. Was it even possible? We were experiencing the greatest sorrow of our lives, but she was experiencing her first moments of pure, untainted joy! She would never have to endure this type of heartache. She would never again feel pain. She had entered her eternal home with her Creator and Heavenly Father. It was a great victory for her, but we were left here to cope with enormous heartache.

Part 1: Our Story Begins

Chapter 1

Kyle and I were married in 1988. We were very much in love, but we lived without a vision and without purpose. Our only dreams were of gaining material possessions. We enjoyed talking about what we would do if we had a million dollars. We would spend hours discussing what we would be able to buy after we acquired good jobs. We dreamed of being able to buy a nice house and nice cars. I was twenty, and Kyle was twenty-five.

Though in love, we were breeding insecurities in each other as we envisioned our materialistic existence. The future we were planning was shallow. We didn't talk about children very often and when we did, it was more about what they would look like and what we would name them. Neither one of us had much, if any, experience with children. We didn't have the ability, at that time, to look at our future child as a person. In our minds eye it was more like another possession that we would gain when we had the money to invest in one, or maybe two.

We both had jobs that paid very little. I was the big

bread-winner at a whopping $6.60 an hour! (This was back in 1989.) We spent most of our money playing. We didn't save any. After a year of eating out, renting movies, and watching television, we knew we needed something more; we were getting bored. That's what happens when you live life for yourself. We were still happily married, although we certainly had our fair share of disagreements. We were just running out of exciting things to do! We began discussing the idea of having a baby.

I had been on the birth control pill for one year when we both had a desire to have a baby. We knew that I should be off of the pill for at least three months before trying to conceive, but before I actually even quit taking the pill, I was pregnant. It shouldn't have been possible, but God was beginning to work in our lives. We just weren't aware of it yet.

It was such an interesting feeling I had when I first became pregnant. It was nothing like I expected. I was nervous and delighted. I immediately fell in love with my baby. I never knew that kind of emotion lived in me. It was wonderful! As my tummy grew, my heart grew desperate to meet the little bundle that I carried. I will never forget the joy of feeling that first kick and that first squirm.

Along with those warm maternal feelings came feelings of responsibility. Kyle and I had discussions about how we were going to raise our baby. What would we tell him or her about God? Did we even understand God ourselves? We called ourselves Christians. If anybody were to ask us, we'd say that we were Christians, but neither one of us really knew exactly what that meant. We knew that we could be saved by believing in Jesus, and we did believe, but there was this issue of sin. I'm not even sure I remember acknowledging that I was a sinner. What was sin anyway? What was I guilty of? It wasn't my fault I was a sinner, was it? I would use the term "saved," but what was I being saved from?

We began to have a desire for a relationship with God. From the time we heard of Jesus, as children, we believed in him, but we hadn't ever truly received him into our lives. During my pregnancy, we both had intimate moments with the Lord when we asked him to forgive us and accept us as his children. We wanted to walk with him and truly know him. When we confessed this to each other, we stood amazed at God's timing. We had both received Christ, and we wanted to know more about who he was. We had accepted Christ, as a little child would, but we wanted to learn about Jesus and teach our child all about him. We had much to learn.

We began going to the church that I had attended as a child with my mom and sisters. My mother had become a Christian when I was in sixth grade. After she came to know Christ, she attempted to introduce him to us. She would read scripture to us, but having never been exposed to scripture before, it was a bit strange, and we didn't like it when mom started 'preaching.' For a short time, Christian music and Christian bookstores enticed me, though I'm not quite sure why. However, it wasn't long before I lost interest and continued in my worldly ways.

Kyle and I now had a sincere desire to learn from God's word. We were thirsty and soaked up each and every sermon. We couldn't get enough! The stories that most people knew well, like David, and Goliath, and Daniel in the lions den, I was hearing for the first time. God was working in our hearts. He was building new desires in us. We wanted to live with purpose. For the first time in our marriage, we had a hunger for holiness even though we were still learning what that meant. We wanted to be a Godly family, but we weren't sure what we needed to do to fit that description.

A few weeks before my due date, I informed my boss that I was going to quit my job and stay home with our baby. She told me that they had discussed promoting me and asked me to reconsider. She used the modern day cliché referring to children, "It isn't the quantity of time that's important, but the quality of time." Kyle and I searched the scriptures for what my role should be as a mother. We read Titus 2 and decided that being a "keeper at home" probably meant just what it said, "at home." How could I be a keeper at home if I was at work? I struggled a little with this, partially because I couldn't see any way we could make it on one small income. But, the conviction was too strong, and besides, I couldn't imagine leaving my baby every day, so we would trust God to provide for us on Kyle's meager salary. It was barely over minimum wage.

We went to our pastor and asked him to pray with us concerning the matter. We told him that we needed a less expensive home. To make ends meet on that income would truly take a miracle. We felt that God was pleased with our desires and knew he would provide, but it did surprise us how immediately he came to our rescue. God immediately responded to our prayers and blessed us in a special way.

A man who had gone to our church (we didn't know him personally) had Alzheimer's disease and had moved to be near his children in Wisconsin so they could take care of him. They weren't prepared to do anything with the house just yet, so they called our pastor to see if he knew anybody who would be willing to live in this home for $100 a month. I think the idea was that having somebody live in the house would lessen the chances of damage or theft. This wasn't a little shack in a bad neighborhood. This was a fairly large brick home with beautiful hardwood floors, two large bedrooms, a nice big kitchen and eating area, and a large living room with a huge picture window overlooking its seven wooded acres! This was far more than we ever would have expected! We enjoyed this home immensely and really grew to love the family that rented it to us. They were doing God's work and they didn't even know what a charity-case we were until they met us!

I wonder what it felt like to be on their end, providing a nice home for a young family in need. On our end, we were experiencing God's provision and rejoicing in it, and on their end, they were meeting a need by God's prompting. It's neat how God uses people at different times, in different ways for his unique purposes!

Chapter 2

Shortly after moving into this home, our first son, Jared Kyle, was born. It was a very long, hard labor, not uncommon for a first baby. I was so exhausted from two days of pain, but I was able to momentarily forget that while I was holding my little darling. He was so adorable with his swollen eyes, pudgy cheeks, and full lips. As a new mom, I just couldn't believe the joy I felt. I had this overwhelming feeling of love. I enjoyed cuddling him, nursing him, letting him sleep in my arms, and even changing his diapers! Only a mother (or the motherly) can understand that. Kyle didn't enjoy the diapers and still doesn't!

I had never spent any time around babies. Most things came natural to me, but there were times I did stupid things from lack of experience. One time I went to a shopping mall with my mom, and we noticed that Jared had soaked through onto his clothes. As we took him to the bathroom to change him, we realized that he didn't have a diaper on! I had forgotten his diaper! This happened twice. My mother teased me mercilessly. I was so embarrassed that when she'd tell people the story I'd get upset, but now I tell the story myself. When I was a new mother I didn't want anybody to know how inexperienced I was, but now that I do have years of experience, I can admit all my silly mistakes. I especially like to tell on myself with new mothers. I'm sure it encourages them in one way or another.

Even with all of the mishaps, Jared survived his first year. He was so fun and truly the center of attention. On my side of the family he was the first child, first grandson, and first nephew. He was beginning to enjoy playing and walking and using little words. We thought it might be time to be thinking about a playmate for him. So, we began to try for another baby.

It didn't take long. In fact, I was pregnant just two weeks after Jared's first birthday. The pregnancy was much different than the first time. I was very sick. I had a feeling very early on that something wasn't right. I couldn't say why and didn't share this apprehension with anybody. It was just a feeling. I consoled myself by thinking that I might be pregnant with a girl and perhaps carrying a girl was different.

As the pregnancy progressed, I noticed that I could feel the baby moving inside of me extremely early. I wondered if I was imagining things. Surely it wasn't possible to feel a baby move at ten weeks. It took nearly sixteen weeks with Jared.

When I went for my pre-natal appointment at about thirty-two weeks, the doctor told me that I was measuring a couple of weeks behind. I worried. I was just sure something was wrong and that this was the first indication. The doctor reassured me that this was very common and that it would just be a good excuse to get another sonogram, (the first one had been very early and fairly uneventful). I tried to tell myself that everything was all right.

The day of the sonogram I was sick all morning from nerves. I just knew that they were going to give me bad news, although I couldn't imagine what it could be. My mom came to pick me up. She was going to go with me and watch Jared. We wanted Jared to be able to see his brother or sister. We met Kyle at the doctor's office. When the technician first started the procedure, she scolded me for not drinking my water. I assured her my bladder was completely full. She said that she couldn't see the top of the baby's head. She continued to look around and then went to get the doctor. The doctor came in and started looking around as he moved the hand-held device across my abdomen. At some point he stopped, turned off the machine, and said to us, "Your baby is very sick." I began to cry. Kyle told the doctor to stop scaring me and to stop making me cry. The doctor then said, "No, let her cry, your baby has a birth defect that is incompatible with life."

There it was. The bomb had dropped, and our world was falling apart. It didn't matter that I suspected something was wrong. Nothing could have prepared me for the sorrow that filled my heart at that moment. I felt sad and scared. None of the details even mattered to me at that moment, I just wanted somebody to take the bad news away and make everything all right.

Our baby had a problem called anencephaly. It is a neural tube defect that affects the development of the brain and skull. Our baby didn't have a brain and was missing the bone on the top of her head. They told us that this was a little girl and that our first daughter was going to die either before, during, or shortly after birth.

The doctor told us that we might want to consider aborting, even at that late stage. I was appalled. We told him we would never abort our baby. He then said that we could go ahead and deliver now so that we wouldn't have to prolong the inevitable, or we could just wait. We were confused and didn't know what to do.

The doctor led me, along with Kyle, Jared, and Mom, to a private room where we could be alone. I wish I could say that I thought to ask God for help, but it was Kyle that gathered all of us together to pray. He gave thanks to God and asked him to help us. After this prayer, we left the office. That prayer got us to the car.

My mom took Jared in her car, and Kyle and I went in his little truck. We didn't say much, but at one point Kyle began to weep so intensely that he had to pull over. I encouraged him to calm down at least until we got home. I felt so sorry for him, but all I could think about was getting home. I wanted to be able to go and be alone with Kyle and just cry. We needed some time to absorb what we were told. It all seemed so strange.

It seemed to take forever, but we finally made it home. We went inside and just clung to one another. We cried and talked and prayed. Even though our baby was still alive, we were mourning as though she was already gone. We weren't sure what was in store for us, but we were willing to let God work and teach us through our first big trial as a married couple.

Our first decision to make was when to have our baby. At first, we decided to wait until thirty-six weeks, which is considered full term. That way if the doctors were wrong, our baby wouldn't be born too early to survive. But as we searched the scriptures for strength and wisdom and asked for counsel, we felt compelled to wait on the Lord to bring the baby in his time, not ours. We decided to just wait and see what happened.

We named our baby girl Abigail Grace. We began to pray for a miracle for our baby. We had read of miracles in the scriptures and had heard people talk about receiving miracles in their lives. Why wouldn't God do that for us and for Abigail? We asked our family and friends to pray for a miracle.

When we first decided to start praying this way, we went to the Christian bookstore to look for a book on miracles and healings. We wanted to hear others stories so that we might be encouraged. There may have been books of this nature in the store, but in our quest, we found no such book. When we talked to an employee that we knew about our sad news she said, "Oh, I want you to meet somebody." She took us over to a lady in the store. This lady was a pastor's wife. She began telling us a story about a lady at her church that had a baby diagnosed in the womb with a major problem, although I can't remember what it was. She said that the people of the church prayed over her, and when her baby was born, it was born with a scar where the problem had been, but that the baby had been healed. She then asked if she could pray for our baby. Right there in the store, she placed her hand on my belly and prayed that God would heal our baby.

She then said that she looked forward to hearing our good news! She said she knew our baby was going to be all right. For some reason, this gave us hope. I felt sure that God sent her to encourage us. At the time, I considered her our prophet. We also called for the elders of our church and asked them to come and pray for our baby. They came over and anointed me with oil and prayed for our baby. They prayed for healing but also asked God to help us to be content with his will if this wasn't his plan for our baby.

I was a bit perplexed about how they prayed, because I felt that if we didn't believe that God would heal our baby, it may not happen. I mistakenly believed that it was my faith that would heal Abigail, not my faith plus God's will.

Until this time in my life, I believed that there were times that God didn't heal and remove conflict in our lives because he had something to teach us, some great plan to work out. I knew that God was capable of healing and removing impossible obstacles from our lives, but I also knew that there were times when he didn't choose to heal and might leave us somewhere we didn't want to be because it was his plan to teach us something and do something wonderful with our lives. I needed to study the scriptures to determine if I believed that God absolutely wanted our baby healed, or if I still believed that God may have a different plan for us.

The scriptures confused me some. I read the verses that said, "...thy faith hath made thee whole," (Matt. 9:22) and "And all things, whatsoever ye shall ask in prayer, believing, ye shall receive.," (Matt. 21:22) but then I also read the verses that said, "...not my will but thine be done" (Luke 22:42) (said by Jesus himself concerning his own painful death), and Paul saying that he prayed three times for his "...thorn in the flesh..." to be removed, but God said, "...my grace is sufficient for thee, for my strength is made perfect in weakness." , (II Cor. 12:7–9). I also read about Moses. God told him to go and speak to Pharaoh and deliver the Hebrew people. Moses told God that he was "slow of speech" and couldn't do it. Then I read, "And the LORD said unto him, Who hath made man's mouth? or who maketh the dumb, or deaf, or the seeing, or the blind? have not I the LORD?" (Exo. 4:11)

I discovered through these and other scriptures that God does indeed withhold healing at times. If God made some people deaf, dumb, and blind, then he also could have made our baby with anencephaly. If God's plan was to heal our daughter then he would, and he would receive glory. But if it wasn't in his plan, then he had something better for us, and he would receive glory then too. I entered into God's rest.

It was comforting to know that it wasn't that I had to believe and not accept the diagnosis. It wasn't my persistence in believing that would make God heal my child. The fear that I struggled with wasn't going to cause God to be mad at me and make him decide not to heal my child. I just had to trust God to work his plan, and I would learn along the way. He knew what was in store for our family. It was not any surprise to him. We still wished we didn't have to endure what was ahead, but we knew that surrendering to God's plan would please him, so we would try to do that.

In my weakness, there would be good days and bad, but as long as I trusted God and daily turned over my fears to him, he would be pleased with me and continue to work on behalf of me, Kyle, Jared, and our baby. I remember saying many times how strange it all seemed. It really was very surreal. This strange new trial took on new meaning when I read the verse in I Peter (4:12–13), "Beloved, think it not strange concerning the fiery trial which is to try you, as though some strange thing happened unto you: But rejoice, inasmuch as ye are partakers of Christ's sufferings; that, when his glory shall be revealed, ye may be glad also with exceeding joy." How interesting that there was even a verse concerning my thoughts on the strangeness of this trial. Apparently God knew that I wouldn't be the only one that would need those words. I hoped that I would be able to rejoice with exceeding joy when this trial came to an end.

I had another struggle during this time: I was losing my desire to continue to carry our baby. I wanted the trial to be over with shortly after it began. I had great fear of the unknown. I found myself not wanting to eat healthy, not wanting to be careful to protect my baby. I was going to lose this baby anyway, what did it matter if I sat on the riding mower and got jiggled a little too much for a pregnant woman. Worst case scenario, I'd go into labor early. The baby was going to die anyway.

When I shared these feelings with a friend of mine who had carried her baby for a few weeks after he had already died, she said, "Lynnette, love that baby while you still have her. She is still alive in your womb. Nurture her and care for her. Sing to her. Love her." I couldn't believe the conviction I felt as I realized how unkind I was being to my child and to myself. I needed to love her and enjoy the precious kicks and wiggles. It was very possible that that's all I would ever have. So, I did. I repented and began to nurture the precious child in my womb. I ate right and took care of myself. I sang to my baby and rubbed my belly and prayed for my unborn little one. I appreciated so much the sweet words of encouragement I received during that difficult time. If she hadn't been so bold to confront me about my error, I may not have ever taken the time to love and nurture the precious child in my womb.

One day at church a friend asked me if I'd ever read Psalm 139: 13–18. I told her I wasn't sure. She shared with me that God made our child fearfully and wonderfully, and that he made no mistakes. She told me to go home and read that passage of scripture after church. I couldn't wait. I opened up my Bible in church and read the passage. Wow! What a wonderful scripture to lift me up!

> For thou hast possessed my reins: thou hast covered me in my mother's womb. I will praise thee; for I am fearfully and wonderfully made; marvelous are thy works; and that my soul knoweth right well. My substance was not hid from thee when I was made in secret, and intricately wrought in the lowest parts of the earth. Thine eyes did see my substance, yet being unformed; and in thy book all my members were written, which in continuance were fashioned when as yet there was none of them. How precious also are thy thoughts unto me, O God. How great is the sum of them, they are more in number than the sand: when I awake, I am still with thee.
>
> Psalm 139:13–18

God knew each part of the special little person that lived in me. He had her life planned even before he began to piece her body together in my womb. He fashioned her, and she was precious in his sight. I began to be truly content in my spirit for whatever God had for us. Kyle and I still prayed for healing for our baby, but we also rested, knowing that he did indeed have a plan and a purpose for this; his creation.

As I carried our baby and faced each day, I fell more in love with my husband. I already knew I had a sensitive, loving man by my side, but this trial in our lives just drew us even closer to each other. We got excited about things God was showing us. We shared our new discoveries with each other. We prayed diligently together. We hugged and cuddled to comfort one another. We suffered together and we grew together. God was strengthening our marriage. Who would've thought that such pain could create such love?

I've heard that trials of this magnitude will often destroy marriages. I can only imagine how hard it would have been without the Lord to strengthen us and help us as a couple. It was our love for each other coupled with our love for the Lord that gave us the ability to be strengthened through the difficult days.

Together we began to see how *our* plan for a perfect family was failing. We had talked about how many children we wanted and how far apart to have them. Everything had been working out exactly as planned...that is, until this happened. If our little one died, it would destroy our plan, and Jared wouldn't have a playmate that was close in age after all. This put a wrench in our spokes and caused some stress.

This disappointment caused us to begin to think about what part God had played in *our* plan. When we realized that God was the giver and taker of life, and no matter how hard we tried to plan, it was really in God's hands, we made the decision to stop planning our family and let God do it. Together we read the scriptures about children. "Lo, children are an heritage of the LORD: and the fruit of the womb is his reward…Happy is the man that hath his quiver full of them….," (Psalm 127:3–5) "…Thy wife shall be as a fruitful vine by the sides of thine house: thy children like olive plants round about thy table." (Psalm 128:3) "Except the LORD build the house, they labor in vain that build it…." (Psalm 127:1). We decided we wanted God to bless us with children in his timing, not ours. If he wanted our quiver full, then he'd fill it, and if not, we would know that it was his will for us.

Being new Christians, this was not something that we had ever thought about, but we truly felt this was something that God wanted us to learn. I think that a part of us was thinking, *We're crazy! What if we end up with ten children?* But we couldn't ignore what God was teaching us, and we were together on it, so we would follow through with what God revealed to us regardless of how insane it seemed. It had been the Holy Spirit and the scriptures that led us to this understanding and conviction, and we are so grateful today for what God taught us then. We may not have learned that if it weren't for the awakening we got through our precious child.

Over time God showed us many people that had trusted God for the size and timing of their family. Some of them shared with us how happy they were to have gained that understanding early on and felt so blessed to have those children that they might not have gone on to have without that learning. We also visited with people that were saddened that they had learned that lesson too late. Those were people who were either beyond child-bearing years or who had surgeries to stop the children from coming. It took a difficult trial to realize it, but we were so glad to have received that instruction from God early in our marriage.

I had some fears about the upcoming delivery of this little one. I was anxious to know whether God had healed our baby or not. When we first got the diagnosis of anencephaly, our doctor showed us a picture of a baby with it. I'm sure his reasoning in showing us this picture was to try to prepare us, but the only thing it accomplished was filling us with more fear and anxious anticipation. The baby in the photos had already died. It was a pathology picture. It wasn't a baby that was wrapped in a pretty blanket and snuggled next to his or her mother. It was very hard to look at this picture. I was so afraid that when my baby was born, I would be as frightened by her appearance as I was by the photo. I couldn't imagine that it would be possible to feel that way about my own baby, but that picture brought with it some serious insecurity. I couldn't get the picture out of my head.

Through a phone call my mom made regarding a support group, I met another Christian lady who had had a son with anencephaly. It was a great encouragement to talk to her. I told her about the picture that I saw, and she wanted to send me a picture of her baby. She thought it might be easier to see, but when I received the picture, even it left me with a discouraged heart. I hate to say that, because I feel so cold-hearted to admit it, but babies with anencephaly are missing the whole top of their head, and it is hard to see that on somebody else's baby and feel prepared to face such a thing. In the picture, her baby boy was in her arms and her husband and two children were by her side. If I hadn't been carrying a baby with anencephaly at the time, I would have thought it was a precious picture, and it really was, but their sweet little baby still looked so different from a healthy one, it made me feel sad knowing that I would have to face it.

In the end, it was helpful in preparing me for what was to come. I did need to see it, and it was a far cry better than the first picture I saw, because it was a personal picture. The love they had for this little boy and the peace that God was giving them was evident in their words and expressions. Talking to this woman did give me some idea of what to expect, so I'm glad that God brought her into my life during that time, if only for a short while.

During this time, a friend of ours recommended that we switch to another doctor; a Christian man. When we called Dr. Watson he said he was happy to take us. We are so grateful for this advice. While there really wasn't a big problem with our first doctor, he wasn't a Christian, and from what we could tell, he didn't value life (no matter how short) like we did. It made a world of difference going to a doctor who would pray with us about the decisions to be made, and who wasn't recommending or supporting abortion as a remedy.

As my due date approached, I began to have many contractions. I knew the day would soon be upon us.

Journal Entry
June 11ᵗʰ, 1992

My darling Abigail, the time for you to come into this world is drawing very near. You are due to be here in nine days. It may be sooner, it may be later…only God knows, and maybe you.

Daddy and I have both had dreams that you are a boy! Wouldn't that be funny if you were after we've called you Abigail for the last two and half months. Well, I'll tell you this, it doesn't matter to any of us if you are! We all love you like crazy! You have brought us much closer to each other and to the Lord.

Your big brother Jared gives you kisses through my belly all the time. I'm sure you know about it because he puckers really loud! He prays for you too. Oh, how that must touch our Lord's heart to hear his prayers. He loves all of us, but I know he must have a special place in his heart for children, because he tells us to have faith like a child, and he never turned children away.

We are anxiously awaiting your arrival. We love

you so much, Abigail. I sure hope you can feel our love for you. I'm just sure you can.

With love,
Your Mommy

The due date came and went. It was two weeks past my due date, and we decided we needed to deliver this baby. When we first got to the hospital, they gave me pitocin. It was successful in starting the contractions, but very quickly our baby began to respond poorly to the contractions. Our doctor told us that our little one was not handling them well and may not be born alive if we continued like this. If we had a c-section, there may be a better chance of seeing her alive. He left us alone to pray about it. We knew that we needed to do everything we could to spare our baby pain and suffering and give us more time with her. So, we chose to have a c-section.

When Samuel Micah was first born, of course our first surprise was that she was a *he!* It wasn't our first daughter, it was our second son! The dreams of our baby being a boy were true!

God had not healed Samuel. He was indeed born with anencephaly, but he was beautiful. I couldn't wait to get my hands on him. Even though we knew he'd only be with us a short while, we celebrated this new life! I was not afraid as I had feared. I was not disappointed. I was excited that my baby was almost ready to be placed in my arms. When he was, I examined every part of him and admired God's handiwork. The only visible problem was with his head. Every other part of him looked like a healthy baby.

My Mom thought of the name Samuel. Thinking of Hannah's Samuel from scripture, it seemed very appropriate knowing that we would have to give Samuel back to the Lord. She knew it would be beautifully appropriate. My mother-in-law gave him his middle name, Micah, which means "Who resembles God." How special to have a son named by his two Grandmas.

You could tell he was two weeks overdue. He was huge! He was only 6 pounds 14 oz, but considering part of his skull and his brain was absent (and a baby's head is very large in relation to his body), you can imagine how big he was. He didn't even fit in newborn clothes! He had Daddy's long fingers and toes. He had slender little lips, more like mine. He had a little hair in the back that was light brown just like Jared's had been when he was born. He was a precious creation of Almighty God! Soon he would be in heaven with his Lord, his Creator, but until then I would love and adore him with all of my heart.

Samuel was held and loved constantly by our friends and family members. We had many visitors in the hospital, because everybody wanted to meet him before he went home to Jesus, and we didn't have any idea how long that would be.

I was able to nurse him a little bit. We were told that he wouldn't be able to feel, see, hear, taste, or smell… that he wouldn't have any senses because he only had a brain stem and no brain. However, this wasn't the case.

He would blink when somebody would take his picture with a flash. He would respond to our touch, and when we tried to give him formula, he would grimace! It made us giggle and rejoice in the little things.

Samuel did have seizures though. When he was having his first seizure, we thought he was dying. He stiffened up from his head to his toes and tightened his mouth and eyes and just stayed like that for what seemed like an eternity, but in reality was probably less than a minute. After it was over, he was fine again. It was frightening. Samuel had several seizures a day. We hated watching him go through them. I cried every time. We discovered that if we covered his head with a hat to keep him warm, he would have more seizures. I'm assuming he had exposed nerve endings on the top of his head, because there was a lot of soft tissue and no bone. This must have stimulated the seizures. So, we kept his head uncovered and just held him close to keep him warm.

We stayed at the hospital just kind of expecting Samuel to die at any moment, but when he was still with us after five stressful days in the hospital, we decided to go home. God was giving us time to get to know our new son, and he was so precious.

We made sure that he was always in somebody's arms. We took turns staying up with him at night, because we didn't want him to die alone, but eventually we just became too tired and decided to let him sleep in the bassinet next to our bed. I would check on him several times a night and try and feed him. He never did eat very well, but he did have a sucking reflex for a few days, so I nursed him when I could and gave him a bottle too so that he could get more nourishment. After about a week of trying to nurse him, we just put him on the bottle. He got to the point where he wasn't able to take enough in, and he lost a lot of weight. His abundance of fat reserves from the womb began to go away. I hated to see him just wasting away. I knew the day was drawing near when we'd have to say goodbye.

On July 14th, 1992, I woke up and looked at Samuel. His color was very ashen. I had never experienced death close up, but I knew when I saw him that he was on his way there. I called our doctor. He told me that it would probably happen within a few hours. It was his day off, and he would come and check on us later.

A few hours passed. My parents were both there with Kyle and me. They were by our side through our bittersweet journey. Jared was there too, but he was taking a nap in the other room. I was grateful for God's timing in that. I remember being a little frightened. I knew Samuel was leaving us, and I was unsure what to expect. However, God gave a gentle peace during those moments.

We took turns holding Samuel. We cuddled him close to us. We prayed together. When I was holding him, he had a seizure. When the seizure was done, Kyle said, "Honey, I think he's almost gone. Let's pray." While Kyle was praying Samuel let out a strange sound, like air being released involuntarily from his mouth, and by the time he finished praying and we all opened our eyes, we realized that Samuel had breathed his last breath. His body continued to make some unfamiliar noises, but we knew that he was with Jesus. "We are confident, I say, and willing rather to be absent from the body, and to be present with the Lord." II Cor. 5:8

When Samuel was alive, we had to be very careful not to hold him too close or too tight, because it almost always made him have a seizure. Now that he was gone, safe in the arms of Jesus, we held his warm body and cuddled him like never before. We kissed him and truly showered him with all the physical love we could. It was a tender moment that we were all thankful for.

Dr. Watson and his wife showed up shortly after that. He confirmed that Samuel was no longer dwelling in his sweet little body, but was with the Lord. We had a friend from church that was a funeral director, and he came and took Samuel. Before he wrapped him up and took him out of our home, I snipped a little bit of his hair off by his neck. I needed a little piece of him to stay with me. That little snippet of hair will always remain in my locket next to his picture.

Up to that day, the hardest thing I ever had to do was place my precious infant son in another's arms, knowing that while I was still alive, I would never hold him again. Samuel had gained heaven, but we were left here with empty arms. God would give us victory, and I would trust in his purposes for all of our pain. I would look forward to seeing Samuel again. This was my first personal experience with death.

Chapter 3

The days following Samuel's death were difficult. My heart felt the pains of death, and my arms craved his sweet little body. I wanted to nourish him with the milk that my body was continuing to produce.

Something in me wanted to reject the peace that God was offering me and instead just sulk and feel sorry for my loss, but at the same time, the pain was so severe that I wanted to escape it. God's peace was right there for me, and I had access to it anytime I reached for it, but I'll admit, there were times when I chose to despair. Why would anybody choose to feel sorrow when they could enter into God's peace? I'm not sure, but I was there at times.

The Bible says in I Thess. 4:13 "But I would not have you to be ignorant, brethren, concerning them which are asleep, that ye sorrow not, even as others which have no hope." Christians should grieve differently than unbelievers, because there is eternity to look forward to. This life is not the end of it all.

Journal Entry
July 16ᵗʰ 1992

My dear Samuel,

You passed away on July 14, 1992 at about 12:25 pm, and I miss you so much. You are with the Lord now though, and I am truly happy about that. That is so comforting to all of us.

Today at 2 pm is your memorial service. I hope you will be able to see us as we remember the thirteen wonderful days we had with you. You were such a cuddly little boy. You loved to be held, and mommy did plenty of that! I had a hard time sharing you, even with Daddy.

I'm so glad I got to nurse you for a while. The Lord was so good to give that to me and you. What a closeness we shared. We brought you to your home on July 6ᵗʰ. You were here in your home with your family for eight days, and almost all of those eight days you did very well. You ate a little, cooed, and even fussed some. We would almost forget that we were going to have to give you back to the Lord so soon. You know, that's why we named you

Samuel. Hannah asked for a child and promised that she would give him back to God. When she had Samuel, she did exactly as she promised. It wasn't something we knew ahead of time, but we too are placing you back in God's hands.

Samuel Micah, we will never forget your short but beautiful life. You will be in my heart forever. I love you so much. You were a precious blessing sent from God and always will be.

Love,
Mommy

I was very pleased with the way the memorial service went. I felt like God was glorified in it, and Samuel was lovingly remembered. I only had one regret following the memorial service; I regretted not having the casket open for the service. While many people were able to meet Samuel while he was alive, there were people that hadn't met him. I wished they would have had the opportunity to see the beautiful little body that held our son. That's all that some people would ever know of him on earth.

When we were making arrangements with the mortuary, they asked us if we wanted to see Samuel after they prepared him for the casket. I was scared and I said, "No." I guess they misunderstood my request, because when we went in to finalize some things with them, they called us back to a room, and there was the open casket on a table, with my precious Samuel lying in it.

Samuel was dressed in his burial clothes (which were

lovingly made by a special friend of ours) and placed in the tiny casket. He didn't look like I expected him to. I'll admit, it was not a joyful moment, but it didn't frighten me as I would have expected. It actually kind of settled some things in me. It made me realize how obvious it was that life had departed from him. He was no longer there. It truly was just the shell that held my little baby. It was like I was looking at a baby doll. Even though there was no life in him, he still looked precious to me. Like I said before, this was my first personal experience with death, and I didn't realize that viewing the body was an important part of adding closure and accepting the death. I know this isn't always possible, but I think it's very important to have this time if you can.

We made the decision to have a closed casket service before seeing Samuel that day, but when I saw Samuel's precious body lying in the casket, I changed my mind. I planned to tell the funeral director that we decided to have his casket open during the service, but because of the thick fog that was over us during that time, we forgot to, so the casket was closed during the service and I will always feel a little disappointed about that.

As I dealt with my pain, I began to realize that there was more to this trial than just heartache. Amongst all the inevitable stages of grief, I also had to learn how to handle others responses to my trial. Many people were doing all the things that I needed, but other people said the strangest things after Samuel died. When somebody has never lost a child or someone they love, sometimes they just don't know what to say. The things I appreciated most were the prayers, the hugs, and the listening ears. We also appreciated meals and financial help. (It's expensive to deal with the "business" of death.)

People quoted scriptures to us verbally and in notes. These were also a great source of comfort, but on occasion, even a verse, was the wrong thing. For instance, a verse like "Count it all joy when you fall into various trials" would probably be better discovered by oneself than received from another.

It might be okay for someone to say, "I wonder how it's possible to count it all joy through our trials, as scripture says." This gives the hurting person an opportunity to reflect on that scripture without being told to do it. Or maybe if someone had experienced that "joy" through their own painful loss, they could truthfully say, "I know it seems impossible, but joy will come, even in the midst of your pain. God's word says it will and I've experienced it." This statement would not be insensitive, because they'd *been there*. It would truly be a word of encouragement coming from someone that had.

Shortly after Samuel died, I remember a pregnant friend being asked whether she wanted a girl or a boy, and she innocently said, "I don't care whether it's a girl or a boy, as long as it's healthy." I knew what she meant. In fact, I myself had said that before. But when you have a sick child die, you don't feel that way anymore. My child, even in sickness, was a blessing in so many ways! I had discovered that blessings come in many different forms. She was innocent in her words, because she hadn't been where I had been, but I've used that story to encourage others to reconsider that phrase. Of course we want healthy children, but we also want God's will for our lives, and there are abundant blessings in things that don't seem good initially.

I know that my friends and family would never hurt me on purpose. It's just hard to know what to say when you're on that side of the trial. Some people feel like they have to say *something,* and it's usually those people that blow it. I learned to appreciate the fact that they were at least trying. Some people (not very many) didn't even do that.

Another real battle for me was fear. Before my pregnancy with Samuel, I wouldn't have considered myself a fearful person. I hadn't faced much tragedy as a child, so I didn't worry about dying or losing someone I loved. After Samuel died, I realized that I was not immune to tragedy. I felt very vulnerable. I feared death at every turn. When Jared got sick, even with a simple cold, I would worry he had a serious illness that would take his life too. I was anxious about every symptom that Jared or Kyle or I had. When I'd drive, I'd be scared I was going to get in an accident. When Kyle traveled by car or plane, I worried. God had taught me so much through Samuel's life and death, but my heartache was still so fresh, I didn't want to have to face death again.

I had a friend who had also experienced loss. She had three babies that had died in early infancy from different problems. She seemed to be obsessed with illness and the details of it. I had wondered about her obsession before I had my own. Was it because she had experienced loss? I had even teased about it (with Kyle), but now I was doing the same thing. The difference was, she would constantly talk about illness and death and about her fears, I just worried inwardly and didn't say anything to anybody, not even Kyle. I feared death secretly, and I hated the fear that consumed me.

Unfortunately, fear will never leave me or anybody else completely until we are with the Lord, but my preoccupation with illness and death did eventually subside. Amongst all the others, this must have been yet another symptom of my grieving. I'm grateful that, like all the other stages, it eventually passed.

It was just twelve weeks after Samuel was born that I found out I was already pregnant. I couldn't believe it! I had gotten pregnant just nine weeks after Samuel's birthday. I was shocked, but I wasn't the least bit disappointed. One of my first emotions was one of fear. What if this baby also had anencephaly? How would I cope? Surely it wouldn't happen a second time, would it? I purposed to set those thoughts aside every time they came to my mind. It's sad how easy it is to learn firsthand of God's love, care, and provision and then turn around and momentarily forget it all for the sake of fear. Fear is a real and terrible thing. "God hath not given us the spirit of fear, but of power and of love and of a sound mind." II Timothy 1:7 We had taught this verse to Jared and he quoted it all the time, but here I was ignoring what I knew to be true. I'm convinced that you can't really learn anything completely until you've experienced it and labored over it. This was going to take some serious effort.

I convinced myself that it would be very unlikely that I would have another baby with this problem. We had been told that our chances of having another baby with anencephaly were slightly higher but that it probably wouldn't happen. Psychology and logic worked temporarily, but reflecting on what God had done and trusting him was the only real way I would gain victory. "Trust in the LORD with all thine heart and lean not unto thine own understanding. In all thy ways acknowledge him and he shall direct thy paths." Proverbs 3:5–6

For some reason, I hadn't been able to gain weight very well while I was carrying Samuel, no matter how hard I tried. I mentally connected that symptom with his problem, so during this pregnancy I determined to gain a lot of weight. I ate way too much, and I didn't get much exercise. I just got fat and out of shape. I gained fifty-seven pounds! My children look back at pictures of me from that pregnancy and say, "Mom, you were so fat!" It was silly logic, but in some strange way, gaining weight helped me emotionally, although it certainly didn't help with the delivery!

We decided to have this baby at home with a midwife. I had never had a completely natural birth and because I've always been into nature and natural health, a natural birth, especially one at home in a more natural environment, fascinated me. Besides, after our experience with Samuel, I had no desire to step back inside a hospital! This delivery would be less than a year following a c-section.

Call it crazy, it probably was, but that's what we felt God was leading us to do, and I was excited.

We had a sonogram seven months into the pregnancy to make sure that things looked all right. Of course we wouldn't have a home-birth if there were any evident problems. The sonogram showed us a couple of things: first, that the baby looked perfectly healthy, which of course brought us great joy, and second, that it was a girl. If they were right, *this* would be our Abigail Grace.

We don't regret our decision to have a home-birth, but it was more difficult than I anticipated. My body was tired and just didn't want to really kick in and do what it needed to do. I labored all day and called our midwife at about ten o'clock p.m. She came over within the hour, but I didn't deliver Abigail until early afternoon the next day. It was a long, difficult labor, but the reward was sweet and fat! Abigail was so cute and so plump! She had a head full of dark, wavy hair, a welcomed sight assuring us that she didn't have anencephaly. All those months of eating too much not only put the pounds on me but on Abigail too! Kyle called her our little Michelin baby. There were rolls and rolls around her tummy and legs and arms.

I never knew a little girl could be so much fun! I always had her in pink dresses and hair bows, anything feminine. She was destined to become a girly girl. I would make sure of that!

Chapter 4

After three pregnancies in three years, and the stress I had endured emotionally and physically, my body got tired. Still, to this day, I don't know exactly what was wrong with me, but I had a challenging year! My usual high energy was gone, and I was struggling with depression due to the frustration of unknown health problems. I was tired all of the time. I always felt spacey. My back ached. My muscles ached. I just wasn't well, but my doctor couldn't figure out what was wrong.

In the midst of all of this, I found out I was pregnant again. What a challenge this would be. Abigail was only eleven months old, and I was so sick. I felt I was being tested on our decision to leave this in God's hands. I was so happy nursing my sweet baby, and now I'd have to quit. I just didn't feel ready for another baby. I didn't think I would be able to handle it physically or emotionally. I was feeling so weak. I confessed my disappointment to Kyle, who had also been very concerned about my health. He told me that he understood, but he knew in time I'd be truly happy and that God would work everything out. He didn't condemn me but prayed for me.

It didn't take long and I was looking forward to meeting this baby and was so glad that God was blessing us again. I felt guilty that I had even felt the emotion of disappointment over the pregnancy, but I knew that it was my human nature and that I had faced enough to justify a few weeks of apprehension. God would understand. Pregnancy wasn't a bad thing for me after all. I had morning sickness for the first three months, but after that my health improved dramatically, and I began to feel good for the first time in over a year. I thanked God for renewing my joy and restoring my health.

We had a sonogram when I was seven months pregnant, and it showed us that this was a baby boy and he appeared to be healthy. The rest of the pregnancy went very well. We had planned another home-birth, but we weren't able to have one because our midwife was facing some challenges in her ministry that took her away from delivering babies for a time. She was a good friend though, and she went to the hospital to help us with the delivery.

The delivery went very well. I could almost say it was a good delivery, but that would be stretching it, because in my opinion, the only good part about having a baby is the baby. Anybody that enjoys childbirth is just plain crazy. I've heard ladies say that the pushing stage feels good. I don't understand that. When I'm at that stage I feel like I'm going insane! I'm usually getting mad at poor Kyle and telling him that I just want to die. I'm rather quiet through childbirth, but I feel frantic and actually try to think of ways to not have to go through with it. I'm really not usually such a baby, but I do hate childbirth. It hurts, just like a curse is supposed to! I *know* it's wrong, but I get a little jealous when I hear of ladies having one or two hours of labor because mine are about thirty-six hours.

Josiah Kent was born at nearly midnight. He, like Abigail, was big and had a head full of wavy black hair. Kyle cut the cord and gave Josiah to me. He was so adorable and so healthy looking, but it was immediately obvious that he wasn't doing what newborns should do. He took his first breath in, let out a little squeal, and then as we waited for his next loud cry, we noticed he was struggling to breathe. Right away the doctor was reaching for him. He quickly took him from me. Before I knew it they were taking him out of the room while squeezing a bag over his face. I told Kyle to go with him. I still had to deliver the placenta.

I felt a bit panicky but tried not to over-react. I just couldn't imagine that there could be anything seriously wrong. He was so big and looked so healthy. He obviously didn't have anencephaly. His head was formed nicely. Surely it couldn't be anything too terrible.

After about an hour, Kyle came back in. He didn't have any news for me, but I could tell he was discouraged. He just had a look about him that told me something was wrong. While I had been assuming that Josiah was fine and would be back in my arms shortly, Kyle had watched the doctors quickly hook him up to a ventilator to help him breathe. He knew it wasn't anything little.

Kyle and I waited anxiously in the room for nearly three hours before we heard anything. Finally a doctor walked into the room. The look on his face made me look away. I wasn't ready to hear what he was about to tell us. He then dropped the bomb. "Your baby is very sick. He has a diaphragmatic hernia. He has a 50/50 chance of survival." I had heard enough. I knew Kyle was there, so I chose not to listen anymore. The details didn't matter to me. All I needed to know, I had heard. I knew there was a chance my son would die. I couldn't believe that God would allow this again. For a moment I screamed out in my heart. *No! This just isn't fair!* It was too much to cope with. My mind went blank as I began to stare out the window. There may have been stars in the sky, but I didn't see them. I just saw the blackness. As I stared, my mind went numb.

As we walked down the hall to go and see Josiah, I remember saying to Kyle, "I can't do this anymore. Two times is just too much. I don't think I can have any more children." For a moment I felt like a rebel. I had an attitude as I walked the halls to the neonatal intensive care unit.

My life was once again turning upside down, and I needed to just deal with what was in front of me, but it would take work. I hoped and prayed that Josiah would be okay. After all, according to the doctor, he did have a fifty percent chance of survival. This was better than Samuel's prognosis. I wouldn't give up. I had to hang on to that hope.

By the time we got to Josiah's bed side, he was already sedated and didn't respond to my touch. I wished I could have felt his little fingers wrapped around mine. It was tough seeing our big, handsome boy hooked up to so many machines. There were tubes and IVs attached to his belly button, his leg, his arm, and going into his mouth. There were so many different sounds; the rhythmic noise of the respirator forcing air into Josiah's lungs and the sounds of alarms and beeps made me feel as though I was in another world. There were chemical odors that made me feel sick.

The doctor told us that when Josiah was developing in the womb, a hole formed in his diaphragm. This caused his intestines to go up through the hole and develop in his chest cavity. His lung on one side was severely underdeveloped. It was the size of a ten week old fetus. He would need surgery at 7 a.m. to repair the problem. We were told the surgery wasn't the hard part. It was the recovery that would be difficult.

The next morning while Kyle and I were back in my room waiting to hear Josiah had come through the surgery, God gave Kyle a special message to lift us both up. Kyle had a cup of coffee in his hand and he said, "God won't bring anything into our lives that he doesn't already have planned." He talked about having victory over fear as we trusted in God's plan once again. He demonstrated this by holding out his coffee cup and telling me to imagine that we were in the coffee cup (empty, of course, not drowning in the coffee), and then he put his hand over it and covered it completely. He said to picture that being God's hand keeping everything out. He said, "God will only take his hand off when he is letting something into our lives. He is protecting us." He used the hymn words, "He hideth my life in the depths of his love, and covers me there with his hand." (He Hideth My Soul, Fanny Crosby) God was speaking through Kyle. It was a sweet moment as we reflected on this God we serve. We knew that we were protected in his care.

The surgery went well. His diaphragm was repaired and his intestines were placed where they should be. However, Josiah's condition was still very critical. His lung was still severely underdeveloped, and there was no way to quickly enlarge it. It would have to grow on it's own over time. Time would tell whether he would recover or not.

I have a tender memory of being alone for a short time and seeking the Lord. I began singing, "Oh how he loves you and me. Oh how he loves you and me. He gave his life, what more could he give. Oh how loves you. Oh how he loves me. Oh how he loves you and me." (Oh How He Loves You and Me, Kurt Kaiser) The words to this song were like a warm embrace. I felt that God was communicating his love to me through this song.

While God was giving me sweet comfort, he was giving Kyle great strength and courage to cling to the promises in his word and share them with anybody who would listen, including each and every person that cared for Josiah. He proclaimed God's love by reading and sharing scripture while standing by Josiah's bed or while visiting with a doctor, nurse, or friend. It was a miracle to see my hurting husband walking around in the spirit. God was obviously doing a great work in his heart.

I still wonder today who may have been touched by this supernatural strength that God was giving Kyle. There was obviously a miracle happening. I couldn't believe it, but I rejoiced, because I wasn't in that same place emotionally and spiritually. I was struggling to keep a good attitude. I was feeling very sorry for myself and was having a hard time understanding why God would ask me to go through this again. I was continually seeking spiritual rest, but I was hurting so badly, and I was discouraged and weak. I was mostly quiet and talked to the Lord in my still moments.

I did marvel and rejoice at the strength that God was giving to Kyle. God used that to bless my heart and lift me up out of my pit. I remember a doctor that continued to write in his medical journal about Kyle's actions. He'd write phrases such as, "Dad is reading scripture to baby" and "Daddy is praying over baby."

On day five, we ran home to freshen up and get some more clothes. While we were at home, I got an overwhelming urge to get back. It hit me very suddenly, so we rushed back. When we got there, nothing was happening. Josiah was still there just as we'd left him. He wasn't doing any better, but he also didn't appear to be doing any worse. We hated leaving him at all, but God's word had reminded me that when we needed sleep or couldn't be with him, he was still with him. God "never slumbers or sleeps." The scriptures come alive during times like these. Many of the verses I had committed to memory came back to me during this time. What a blessing to hide God's word in our heart. It's not always easy or convenient to open the Bible and read it, especially during a time of such stress, but what a blessing it was to have verses come to mind without even searching for them.

Sometime late in the evening a nurse came into our room woke us up and said, "Josiah isn't doing well. You better come right away." We were sleeping in a room that they had set up for parents of critically ill children. We quickly went to Josiah. When we walked in, we noticed the doctor was standing over him. He told us that he was going into respiratory arrest. We stood there for a while just staring at our son.

After a few minutes, we saw what was happening. Josiah was still in a drug-induced coma, so there was no physical change that we could see, but the machines showed us what his body was doing. While we watched the numbers and listened to the alarms, his heart had stopped beating. The doctor did chest compressions and bagged him. Josiah's vitals stabilized for a few moments, but then it happened again. The doctor told us that he expected Josiah to die. He said, "I can continue to resuscitate him, but I really think we are prolonging the inevitable. There really isn't any more we can do."

We didn't say anything, but instead just stood there and watched as the doctor tried to resuscitate Josiah again and again. Finally when he asked for permission to stop, we said yes. It was, obviously, Josiah's time to leave this earth. My heart cried out to God. The hope I had for his life to remain was now gone.

Surprisingly, a song of victory immediately came to my mind immediately after Josiah died. The words that came to mind were:

"The angels are singing again.
Ten thousand hallelujahs begin.
The heavens resound,
the lost has been found.
The angels are singing again!"

-Ron Hamilton

It is a song of deliverance and that was what Josiah had just received. He had been delivered from this world so full of sin. He would never be tempted to sin. Yes, he had the sin nature that every man by inheritance is born with, but he would never choose sin! Hallelujah!

As I stood trying to take it all in, I truly marveled that I was staring at the lifeless body of my five day old son and feeling as though I didn't want to face tomorrow, yet God was giving me a song to give me perspective.

Somehow I could say, "Hallelujah!" in my spirit, in the midst of my sorrow.

I must confess a strange thing at this point. I kept thinking and hoping that when they took the tubes out of Josiah's mouth, he would just start breathing…it was unrealistic, but I hoped for that. Josiah didn't come back to us. We were happy for our son. He was in the presence of God. He was with his brother Samuel. Kyle kept repeating the verse, "To live is Christ and to die is gain." (Phil 1:21) He was perfect and whole, but once again, we suffered. We would have to go home without our precious son, Josiah Kent.

Sometime during Josiah's last moments, my mom came and stood by our side. My dad stayed behind to be with Jared and Abigail. Our pastor also showed up and two other dear friends. We had named Josiah Kent after our pastor, Kent Holcomb. He had been a good friend and a Godly influence in our lives.

We all stood around Josiah for a while. I told them about the song that had come to mind and Pastor Holcomb said, "That very song came into my head too!" It was a song that we had recently sung at church during our Christmas cantata.

We all held Josiah. Our tears dripped on his precious little body. The only other time I had been able to hold Josiah was seconds after his birth. Now I was holding him minutes after his death.

We weren't sure how we'd walk away from Josiah that

night, and we weren't sure what to do next, but we said good-bye. Our big, handsome, dark-haired boy would not cuddle up and nurse, would not play guitar with Daddy, and would not grow up in our home with his brother and sister. We would enjoy him someday, but not yet. I'm not sure how much I longed for heaven before, but my longing was greatly increasing. I was looking forward to the day that my Lord would take us all to be with him. I found myself wishing that we could all go right then! I didn't want to feel the pain. I just wanted relief from the sorrow.

The days and weeks that followed were very difficult for me. I really struggled with sadness. We should have been a family of six, but we were a family of four. I became discouraged. I was leaning very hard on the Lord.

I woke up early every day so that I could be alone and be comforted by the scriptures before Jared and Abigail got up. I got my cup of coffee and sat at my kitchen table. The sun warmed me as it shined through my east-facing windows. I desperately needed God to give me comfort and hope. I read the Psalms constantly. In fact, I read at least five a day, this way I would read all the Psalms in a month. The Psalms have always been a great source of encouragement for me when I'm facing something that seems impossible. In fact, I hate to admit it, but I've leaned on the Psalms through so many difficult times that when everything is okay in my life, I usually don't go to them because they remind me of the sad times. Maybe someday that will change.

I was hurting and struggling, but I was growing. I was growing in my desire to serve Christ. I was growing in my desire to trust him and accept his plan even if I didn't understand it. I was growing in my love for Jesus. Oh how I loved him. I felt so undeserving of this comfort he was giving me. Every single time I sought him, he was there. He was faithful to his word. He never left me in my sorrow and depression. His words gave me hope and escape from my sorrow every time I read them and meditated on them.

A friend of mine came over to visit one day. We were most likely drinking coffee out of pretty teacups and eating homemade shortbread or pound cake, something we did almost every time we got together. I was explaining to her how I had struggled more this time with ongoing sadness. I told her that I didn't understand why God would make me give back two sons. She said, "If God said to you, 'Lynnette, I would like to give you a son. He won't be with you long. I am only going to leave him with you for five days and then I'm going to take him back, but I have a plan. Will you accept this assignment?'" She then said, "I know you'd say, 'Yes, Lord, I'm your willing handmaiden.'"

I had never thought of it like that. If God *had* asked my permission, would I have said yes? I thought about it for a while and decided I would! I would do anything to please the Lord, even if it meant pain and sorrow. At least I hoped I would. That truly was my heart's desire.

I wanted to serve Christ in whatever way he wanted me to. It gave me courage to look at it this way. I wanted to be willing to do anything for my master. It shed some new light on this trial I was trying so desperately to get through. Yes, I would pretend that God had asked me to endure this trial, and I had said yes. It made it just a little easier to bear, acting as though I was a servant completing a task for my loving master. In essence, that's really what it was.

As God healed my sorrow, I not only grew in my desire to live a holy life that pleased Christ, but I also found myself grateful that I was in a position to help others. Surely after my heartache people would hear me. I wanted to proclaim God's healing power and his loving kindness and display my own life as one that was not over or ruined because of sorrow but was better because of it.

I knew that this great sorrow that my family was called to endure was ordained by God, and we would once again be victorious! "I know, O Lord, that thy judgments are right and that thou, in faithfulness hast afflicted me," (Psalm 119:75).

Chapter 5

The next six months were interesting. While he had taught us so much already, God still had much more to teach us. The Bible is so full of instruction and hope for Christians. It is a never-ending book of lessons.

Through our trials and our growing love for our Lord, the Kraft family seemed like a pretty strong unit. We had learned to depend upon one another and support each other through some very difficult days. Perspective was something that truly changed for me and Kyle, and we felt we were able to look at life through different eyes. We felt better equipped to face challenges, but as I said before, God doesn't work in our lives and then just quit. In fact, I think that when God begins to work and he sees a willing vessel (and sometimes even when we're not willing), he just keeps working!

One thing I learned early on about my husband is that he likes people. He enjoys encouraging others and making them smile. I guess you could say he's often the life of the party and the center of attention. It must come from being the baby of his family. I've often thought of myself as a people person and somewhat outgoing but not compared to him.

I'm sure it's because of Kyle's fun personality and his love of teaching that we were asked, as a couple, to help lead the College and Career group at church. It sounded like something that would be fun, and we loved the other two couples leading it, so after discussing it, we decided we would do it. One thing I noticed very quickly was that I wasn't really that important to this ministry. Who they really needed was Kyle. He would be somebody that could teach the Sunday school class and build relationships with the students. I was busy managing our two young children, so I never really contributed much beyond just being a support to my husband, but I do believe that that alone is a valid and worthy ministry.

We had been to some parenting classes and felt we had learned (from scripture) what our children needed, and we were trying very hard to do the right things. We were teaching our children about Jesus and teaching them to behave and to be kind. Kyle spent a lot of personal time with Jared and Abigail. He would do skits with them (usually Bible stories), and they would video tape themselves all dressed up in robes and turbans (towels) and such. He would also get down on the floor and build huge Lincoln log forts, and he would read Bible stories to them every evening.

Kyle had a great job and was supporting us financially,

and this allowed me to stay home to teach, love, and care for the children and our home. Yes, we were making many mistakes, but our hearts desire was to give it our all and to please the Lord in our parenting.

We had assumed that God would want us to be involved in any church ministry or activity that we could, but the College and Career ministry we were involved in was making things very hard at home. Kyle spent so many hours preparing for his Sunday school class that he was too tired to even read a simple Bible story to the children. These College and Career students weren't the easiest to teach. They were at an age and stage in life where they had more time to devote to study, and they loved to ask Kyle difficult questions that he didn't always have the answers to. I'm not saying that nobody could keep up and perform well in a situation like this, but most people wouldn't be able to keep up with a family, a full time job with travel, household chores, and teaching. Consider what a huge job just the first two are!

He was also traveling two nights out of the week with his job and began to get very overwhelmed with life. Right when we felt like we had a pretty good hold on our family and things were going well, something began to change almost without notice. Life became much more stressful for me. I noticed that we were not spending as much time together as a family, and Kyle wasn't spending near as much time with Jared and Abigail. Jared and Abigail had me every day, all day long, but Kyle was just becoming too busy to spend much time with them.

It wasn't that he was absent all the time, but when he

was home, he was down in the basement or veggin' out in front of the television because he was just so tired. I became aware of the change and Jared did too. Jared was at an age where he was capable of taking in and learning so much. Jared, being a first born, had spent a lot of time around adults and fit in quite well! He was a good reader, writer, and communicator. He was very aware of the change in our family and often said so. Abigail, being two, was at the age where she was just mostly into mischief. I would often find her in the bathroom putting on makeup or drinking toilet water or outside decorating the yard with flower petals from all the flowers that she pulled from my garden. She learned to walk when she was ten months old and was ready to conquer the world from that day forward! She was definitely in need of her daddy's loving influence and firm hand!

Yes, Kyle was being missed by me and by the children. Admittedly, I grew bitter. My frustration was with Kyle, but it was also with the church and even the college and career-aged young adults. I was disappointed that after all we had been through together Kyle wasn't being a better spiritual leader in our home. He was growing so much in his love for God and his word and he wanted to read it, study it, and share it. That was a wonderful thing in and of itself, however, he often said, "I just can't teach on a child's level." As a wife, I grew weary trying to do it all. I knew if I continually brought it up, he'd grow bitter against me, his nagging wife. I was perplexed and didn't know what to do. I didn't want him to stop studying and teaching, but I wanted him to come down a few levels and spend time in the Word with us, his family.

When I was newly pregnant with another baby, and I'll tell you about her very soon, Kyle went to camp with the College and Career group. I couldn't go because I was sick with the pregnancy and because I had the two children to care for. He took vacation time from work and went on a several day trip to Colorado. I missed him and continued to grow bitter inside. I wanted him to be as devoted to us as he was to this group of young adults. He was very popular in this group. The students loved him. In fact, when they got back from camp, they publicly awarded him "Camper of the Week." If he hadn't had such a consuming job, maybe this ministry would have been an acceptable one, but with his travel and busy job, it was too much for him. Like I said, we were still trying to figure out how to be parents and now he had about twenty-five older students to devote his time to as well.

One day at church I remember sitting in the pew with the children waiting for Kyle. Sunday school had just finished and the worship service was getting ready to begin. As the service started, I left the children with my mom and went to search for Kyle. I couldn't find him anywhere. I went and sat down and fell apart inside. I was upset that the church had my husband and I didn't. When he finally came in, about twenty minutes into the service, I was so upset I couldn't even look at him. I held it in and didn't say anything. *If only he would communicate with me.*

Why does he feel it is my responsibility to always watch over our children and somehow it's his responsibility to teach and encourage children that aren't ours? Why doesn't he have the common courtesy to tell me where he is going to be? This had happened on more than one occasion. I wanted us to be raising our children together. He had been such a good daddy and loving husband, but as he got more involved in church our family weakened. His knowledge of scripture was increasing, but the application of it regarding his family was lacking and our family was suffering. The bond wasn't as tight as it had once been.

I've read and heard many stories about men in full-time ministry that win many to the Lord but also lose their children and often their wives in the process. It is difficult for a man (or woman) to perform his God-given duties and not fail somewhere. For Kyle, the ministry wasn't his full time job it was a part time one. He already had a full time job and was extremely busy with it. At this stage in our lives, it just wasn't possible to do it all. When talking to my children, I often use the old saying, "A job worth doing is worth doing well." For Kyle, it was impossible to do every job well. There was too much pressure trying to balance several days of travel a week, a full time job, house chores, his young children, his young (and frazzled) wife, his ministry, his extended family and friends, and his personal time with the Lord.

One Sunday we were getting ready for church, and I was dreading another Sunday. It had begun to be a burden in many ways, but more than anything, church reminded me of my missing husband! We were supposed to be leaving for church, and I just burst out in tears. Kyle asked me what was wrong. Everything that had been on my heart for weeks just spilled out. It had been bottled up for too long. He called the church and told another College and Career leader that he knew it was last minute, but he'd have to cover for him. Kyle and I talked and talked and talked. I told him we'd been through so much together, but what good was it all if our marriage and family fell apart. I needed him. The children needed him. He was our leader and we desperately wanted to be led.

He immediately responded to my pleas and told me that he knew for some time he had been neglecting his family. He explained how easy it is to get caught up in intellectualism and popularity and forget to just do what you know God wants you to do. He knew he was failing in his God-given task of leading his family. He was willing to step down from the ministry so that he could resume that post.

Not everybody was happy about it. The students in that class loved Kyle! But I was happy, and the children were happy. I was so thankful that my husband was humble enough to admit his mistake and was ready to resume his post being a Godly father and husband who "Brings them up in the nurture and admonition of the LORD." (Eph. 6:4)

I often wonder why churches don't utilize the elders more for ministries. It seems that it's the young fathers that are often recruited to lead ministries, especially those with young people, and so many of them are just not ready to do it, yet the pressure is there. The elders in the church are perfect for these ministries. Not only are they seasoned in life, but they usually have more time to spend in these ministries without giving up another important role.

I do regret that I didn't lovingly confront Kyle earlier, before the bitterness set in. It wasn't a long trial, being less than a year, but I'm sure it could have been a much shorter one had I responded in the correct way. Kyle hadn't set out to do the wrong thing. He just got in over his head before he realized it. I know that he would have stepped down much earlier had I just said something.

Six months after Josiah's birth and death, another child was in my womb. This child would be baby number five. I struggled at times with uncertainty, but God gave me peace and filled me with excited anticipation through the pregnancy. We now had two babies in heaven, each having been born with unique, unrelated problems. In my flesh, I was tempted to worry, but my spirit was content knowing that God had helped us through the deaths of two children and was stretching us and showing us new things we couldn't see before. I asked myself, *what's the worst thing that can happen?* I knew from experience that God could even comfort us in the death of our child, but my arms longed to embrace this child. My heart longed to nurture this little one. I hoped and prayed daily that God would allow us to keep this precious baby. Losing two in a row might just be more than I could bear.

The months during my pregnancy were precious for my family. They were healing months. Kyle was present again and teaching us and loving us with his time and attention. We grew very close. Not only was Kyle spending time truly having fun with all of us, but he was also leading and teaching at a level the children could understand and enjoy. He would sit on Abigail's bed and read out of *The Child's Story Bible* (Catherine F. Vos) every night. They loved that time with Daddy and have fond memories of those times.

Everybody was looking forward to this next baby's arrival. Nine months quickly passed. When I was pregnant with my first and even second child, nine months seemed like an eternity, but when I became pregnant with later babies, I found myself grateful for the time to prepare for the new baby. I wasn't in such a hurry, that is, until the last few weeks, when I'm so uncomfortable I can't stand, sit, lie down, walk, tie my shoes, etc.

When the time to deliver drew near, I had contractions for a few days. I knew from past experience not to go to the hospital too soon. I have very long labors and nothing ever progresses quickly. When I went for my pre-natal appointment at thirty-nine weeks, my doctor told me I was dilated to five! I couldn't believe it, I was halfway to being fully dilated, and I wasn't even in active labor. I shared my fears with him about the delivery. It's hard to get yourself ready for a tough labor and delivery when all you can think about is whether the baby is going to be healthy or not. I was so preoccupied with these thoughts that I was having trouble revving up for all the pain to come! Our doctor, who knew us quite well by then, had compassion and said he would help me out. He had a plan to get me an epidural after admitting me, and then he'd come and break my water since I was already dilated to five.

The nurse at the hospital thought it was a little strange when I told her that Dr. Jensen said I could have my epidural when I wasn't even having regular contractions, but Dr. Jensen was very familiar with how my deliveries were and knew I'd kick in once my water was broken (I've always delivered rather quickly after that), so he gave the okay. It was all so easy, I almost felt guilty! I went into the hospital around 5:30 p.m. I had my epidural within the hour; my water was broken about an hour after that. I visited with Kyle and my family for a couple of hours, and then I took a nap for about an hour. I woke up with a lot of pressure. I knew I was ready to deliver. The nurse came in and said I was completely dilated. Our doctor, who had been roaming around the hospital waiting for me to deliver, came in and got ready for the delivery. When it was time to push, I pushed one time and her head came out, then another time and the rest of her was born. It was our sweet little Cecily Kate. She was our smallest baby at seven pounds and only nineteen inches long.

She was so tiny and adorable. We had a little scare because she had wet lungs, but after a short while, they reassured us that she was fine. My parents and Jared and Abigail came in and saw her. We all held her, cuddled her, and adored her. As you can imagine, we were rejoicing! We stopped to pray and thank God for this blessing. Jared, our 5 ½ year old, asked if he could pray. We, of course, said "Yes." He began, "Dear Heavenly Father. Thank you for our baby. Please help her not to die tomorrow. In Jesus' name, Amen." It became apparent to us at that moment how hard our sorrows had been on our young son. Jared had suffered in his own little boy way. He had been more aware of what had happened than we had even realized. We were so glad that God was leaving Cecily here, for us *and* for our children. We had the video camera on a tripod recording when Jared prayed. We captured on video this sweet child crying out to the Lord to spare the life of his sister. I wonder what kind of feelings that video would stir up in him today. Would he remember what emotions he had that day? He was only 5 ½ years old then, but how many children this age have had to watch two brothers die. I was twenty-four before I ever lost anybody that I was close to, Jared was a tiny child. God was working in his life at such a young age. The Lord doesn't only consider adults when going through trials, he walks with his little children too, and he works in their lives as abundantly as ours. Jared's understanding may not have been clear, but that was all the more reason to need the comfort and love of Jesus to heal his broken heart.

So often our children get lost in the shuffle of life. Sometimes they don't even know what questions to ask during a family trial because it's just all too difficult for them to grasp. It's a comfort to know that the Lord is right there with them. We know, according to scripture, that he has a special place in his heart for children. These times are not only an opportunity for *us* to grow in faith and love for our Savior, but it's an excellent time for our children to grow too. The Bible says that Timothy knew the Holy Scriptures from the time he was a child. We need to be teaching them to our children, no matter how young they are. No child is too young to hear the scriptures. No child is too young to be comforted by Jesus. He is real in our lives. He is real in theirs. If we turn them toward Jesus through hard times, they will learn to turn to him themselves someday.

We all enjoyed Cecily so much. I would pick her up at 5 a.m. and take her downstairs with me to study the Bible with Kyle. Kyle was teased because he held her so much. We all had a hard time sharing Cecily with anybody, even with Grandma and Grandpa. When you've tasted the pains of death, it's easier to remember to see the little things and take time to make memories and enjoy one another. The little things in life are truly some of the most wonderful things to notice. The heart never rids itself of the one you love, they will always be with you and there will always be a little twinge of loneliness for the one that you don't have with you, but you have to move on and in moving on, you search for greater purpose and more beautiful insight.

What some people might consider boring days are just great for someone who's faced a crisis. At least a boring day means there is no crisis. It's kind of the same feeling as having a baby. You go through the horrible trial of labor (in my opinion). You think you're going to die from the pain (again, my opinion). Then, when the baby is born, even though you're still not very comfortable, compared to the horrible pain you've just endured, you feel content. That's what I felt on a humdrum day—contentment.

Chapter 6

When Cecily was just a few weeks old, the company Kyle worked for dissolved all the positions in Wichita from his department. Without warning, his job was taken from him. He was given a severance package that paid off most of our debts, which was a huge blessing. (We had never even heard of a severance package, and we were very pleased when we realized what one was!) However, we still had to make a house payment and pay for utilities, gasoline, food, and other daily needs without an income and with no savings whatsoever.

Kyle tried very hard to find a job, but since he was not having any luck finding one, he began brainstorming a business idea. He's always had an entrepreneurial mind. I, not being quite the risk taker, have often tried to talk him out of his ideas, but this one I couldn't talk him out of. He decided to go for it and start up this new business: a commercial waste and recycling, brokerage company. He had been working in that field for quite some time and had learned a lot about it and truly enjoyed the business.

When he made the decision to start the company, he decided to hire somebody immediately to take care of office work and customer service because he had to get on the road and sell. It would have been helpful if I could have done this for him, but having three young children to care for made it impossible for me to be much help.

He had a couple of investors that were willing to go out on a limb because they trusted Kyle and his abilities (or maybe it was just because they loved him and wanted to help him). The business appeared to be one that would do well eventually. However, because it was a slow start, there wasn't enough revenue to pay the one employee or Kyle for that matter. During this time, Kyle was offered a sales job from an Atlanta company. He would be able to work from our home, but he would also have to travel some. We both saw this as an answer to our prayers, because he wouldn't need to take a salary from his business if he had one offered elsewhere. He worked both jobs for a few months, which was really too much for one person, but after a very short time the Atlanta company changed ownership and he lost that job too.

What appeared a good idea in the beginning was proving not to be such a great idea after all. Things were not going as planned. It was obvious some changes would need to be made. Here we were again with no income and his company was not yet where it needed to be to sustain itself. The investor's money had run out and neither one of us wanted to ask for more. We were already $40,000 in debt to the investors, and we were frightened at the idea of going in deeper. The business plan was good, but there just weren't funds to support the start-up, and it was quickly losing ground financially. It appeared the business would fail.

He wasn't sure where to go with it or what to do next. At this point, he went to a business acquaintance to seek advice and possibly get some help. This was a man he'd met on an airplane about a year prior, and he'd seen him a couple times since. This man showed interest in the business, and before we knew it, he was making Kyle an offer to fund it. The catch was that he would be the majority owner, not Kyle.

This meant that the business could survive, but it wouldn't be Kyle's business any longer. It appeared to be his only option. At this point he was tempted to just pull out of the business and count his losses, but the investment money was in the forefront of our minds. We were so grateful for these friends and family members who were so willing to believe in Kyle and his business. We knew that if he closed the doors, these generous people whom we loved would suffer a loss too. We were also concerned that it would put a strain on our relationships. We knew it would be a long time before we'd be able to pay them back, and it was likely we'd never be able to. So, in desperation, Kyle made the decision to become a business partner with this man—an unbeliever.

At first, it appeared to be a good set up, but it didn't take long for Kyle to realize that it was a huge mistake that he had made. This other man had the upper hand in everything, and he wasn't a pleasant man to work for. He instructed Kyle to fire his employees (he had hired another person shortly after the partnership began) and told him that they were both inadequate. These were both friends of ours, and it put great pressure on our friendships. He was also going to make other changes that Kyle didn't agree with. Kyle was asked to make compromises and do things he just didn't feel right about. This man seemed to be there to help, but in time we both realized that he was looking for a good business deal. He wasn't interested in friendship.

This new business plan created a huge amount of stress in our lives, especially Kyle's. I will never forget this time. In some ways it was worse than when our babies had died because that was completely in God's hands, and we had no control over it. We were suffering together through those trials. In this situation, Kyle knew that we were suffering because of poor decisions he had made, and he had a great amount of guilt. He had to just see it through. No matter what he lost along the way, he just needed to get out.

It turned into such an ugly mess that Kyle had to get legal counsel from an attorney friend. There was a point when Kyle sat in his office discussing matters with this man, and he kicked Kyle out of his own office. Kyle began to gather his personal belongings and he told Kyle to put everything down. He wouldn't even let him take his radio out of the office. No, this business was no longer an exciting adventure. It had become one of the greatest stresses of our lives,' and it would not be easily fixed.

Eventually, after a long battle, with money lost and lives burdened, the business that Kyle developed and worked so hard at was completely overtaken by his partner. We, and those who had invested in Kyle and his company, lost. Kyle's business continued on, but he no longer had part in it. I suppose this man knew what he was doing when he offered to fund Kyle's business. He was a smart businessman, but I doubt he had very many friends.

It was very hard on our marriage. There was no peace for Kyle. He wouldn't receive words of encouragement from me. He didn't feel we were in it together. It wasn't a selfish heart he had but one full of regret and guilt. He refused to be comforted. I hated to see his courage and strength gone.

God's children always have a reason to hope. He always shows us a way out. I believe the first step to healing and restoration is repentance. It's at that point that he pulls us out of our pit and puts us back on solid ground. Kyle did repent and asked God to show him what to do next. God was there to pick Kyle up and put him back on the correct path.

We eventually got through that difficult trial. It took a lot of work! Kyle was wounded, but not defeated. He spent a lot of time with our attorney and lost, all the way around, but at some point he could put it behind him and simply say, "I will never do anything like that ever again!" The negative feelings that the business failure created eventually did subside, but friendships were severely wounded. That would take more time to heal.

The scripture says not to suffer as an evil-doer, but if you suffer as a Christian, "happy are ye." No wonder this trial was so difficult! Kyle wasn't evil per se,' but he also wasn't suffering because of doing good or being righteous. He was suffering because of poor choices, and he fell very hard. In time though, he was better for it. I guess you could say he learned the hard way and will be able to share the wisdom he learned with our children and grandchildren and anybody else that God may put in his path that could benefit from his failed business story. I hope I never have to see the man I love in that sort of bondage ever again.

Perhaps someday God just might give me an opportunity to sympathize and pray for a young wife in similar circumstances. What is life without stories of our failures and victories? Hopefully, as Christians, every one of our failures will end up as victories!

We had come to the point where the business was behind us. That was good, but here we were once again.... unemployed and broke! Only this time was a bit more stressful, because we discovered that I was expecting another baby. Sweet blessing number six. Timing? Well, in my opinion, it could have been better, but of course I knew that it must be perfect since God had placed this child in my womb. How would we ever really learn to trust and obey him if we weren't tested and tried? God knew exactly what we needed. He knew how stubborn we were and how much we needed to endure to really learn to appreciate his plan and leave things in his strong and capable hands.

We did have a cost-sharing plan to help with medical bills, but it was expensive and we weren't sure how we would keep it with no income coming in. But, how would we ever be able to deliver a baby without some sort of financial assistance? If we could have a home birth that would help, but having had two children with serious medical conditions, we weren't sure we wanted to put a midwife or ourselves through that kind of stress or risk our child's life.

Kyle began to look for work again. He started to do some contract work for a local box company. The job was only temporary, and because it was contract work, we didn't receive any company benefits, like medical insurance, but at least we had something to work with! We were very grateful for God's provision.

The babies that had problems were numbers two and four. I was expecting baby number six. Would this baby have a problem because it was the next even-numbered one? We hoped there was nothing to this number pattern, but we wondered.

The pregnancy started a little rough. In the first trimester I was horribly sick with the flu, but other than that, it was going well. I wasn't terribly affected by morning sickness as I had been with some of the others. I wasn't anticipating problems. Yes, we had had two problems with two of our children, but we were told they were unrelated, and we were also told that neither one was genetic. However, there was that constant, nagging fear that had permanently settled way down in the deepest part of my being and attempted to come to the surface on a daily basis. I knew this anxiety and fear I felt were both sin, and I tried so hard to put them back where they needed to remain. God was real in my heart and life. I knew that this fear wasn't from him. When I considered his greatness and his loving kindness, I didn't fear. When I considered the pain I'd endured and pictured myself with empty arms again, I did.

When I was about seven months into the pregnancy, it was time for a sonogram. This had become routine for us. We didn't want to have a sonogram too early and discover a problem early on only to have to wait months for the outcome to play out, but we didn't want to avoid a sonogram all together only to discover a problem after delivery that could have been treated or handled more carefully had it been diagnosed ahead of time. So, we scheduled a sonogram.

As usual, I couldn't eat very much the day of the sonogram. I was nervous. I always get so mad at myself for not resting in the Lord. What is there to fear when you know that your steps are ordered by the Lord? I knew that God had made this child fearfully and wonderfully. I wish I was a spiritual giant and could just truly rest in him all the time. I think of the verse, "Come unto me, all ye that labor and are heavy laden, and I will give you rest." (Matthew 11:28)

I often find myself quoting the verse, "...the spirit indeed is willing, but the flesh is weak." (Matthew 26:41b) That is how it is! I want to serve God and do anything he asks of me, but the anticipation of things that are out of the ordinary scares me. I like my comfy little world with everything where *I* want it.

As the sonogram began, I tried to get through it by talking a lot. I was a nervous wreck. I decided to confess my anxiety to the technician so that she could talk me through everything and help me through it. I was afraid I was going to be sick, so I thought I might as well confess, just in case I had to hop up and run out of the room. She was sympathetic and tried hard to be open and honest with us and say what she could. She visited with us as she looked around inside my belly. I was encouraged when we could see the nicely formed head. I was encouraged when she showed us the diaphragm and told us it looked good. At some point though, she got quiet. I noticed she was turning her head sideways and had a perplexed look on her face. After what seemed like an eternity, she said that the stomach appeared to be on the right side instead of the left. My mind began to race. I attempted to prepare myself for whatever was wrong. I had never experienced the news, "the stomach is on the right side." What did that mean? She left to get the doctor. In my heart and mind I began to cry out to God in fear as we waited for her to come in. I don't think Kyle and I said anything to each other. What was there to say?

When the doctor came in, she began to ask us questions about our other children. She talked to us as she looked at this little one that we had just been told was a girl. The first information she gave us was that her stomach was definitely on the wrong side. Then she looked at the heart very thoroughly and only saw two chambers. She also told us that it was only a two vessel cord which is often associated with birth defects.

This doctor was about as grim as they come! She didn't even try to give us good news. From what she saw, she knew something was wrong, but she gave us the worst case scenario about everything. She told us that this combination of problems could indicate a serious chromosomal defect, and we should consider having an amniocentesis to determine that. She said that if it was the kind of defect that she suspected, we may want to abort. If we didn't want to do that, we would at least want to know so that I wouldn't have an unnecessary c-section just to save a baby that may not have any quality of life. I was shocked at her comment (and her coldness). Why did she decide to go into this type of work? Did it thrill her to give people bad news?

As I think back, I pity this woman. I can't imagine living with such a negative spirit. I enjoy giving people words of encouragement and hope. She seemed to somehow enjoy giving bad news. She didn't treat us like people. I felt like we were the result of some failed experiment. My heart was hurting as I was dealing with this news, and she didn't even try to soften the blow. For some doctors, I understand it must be hard to have to give parents that kind of news. I imagine these doctors harden themselves a little so that it isn't so hard on them emotionally. However, I didn't get that feeling from this doctor.

When we were with her, the situation seemed

hopeless, and we were discouraged. Would our little girl live or die? What was wrong with her? What would we tell our children who were at home with Grandma? My mom is so sweet and tender, how would she take the news? She not only hurts for herself, but she hurts for us, her children. She had been right by our side through each and every trial. Jared was almost eight now, and above all, I couldn't imagine having to break the news to him. He was so excited to hear the news of this baby. How would Abigail take hearing that her baby sister may not live?

We left the office and decided that we wouldn't use the cell phone. We didn't want our voices to give anything away. We wanted to tell them in person. We didn't really know what to say exactly. All we knew was that something wasn't right with her heart and that her stomach was on the wrong side. We would have to wait to find out more from the pediatric cardiologist who would do an echocardiogram two weeks later. The wait seemed like forever.

When we walked in the door, my mom and Jared and Abigail were all at the kitchen table eating leftover pie. They looked at us and my eyes gave it all away. I just said, "Well, something is wrong with this little one too. Oh, and it's a girl." Kyle and I told them what we knew, which seemed inadequate to them and to us. Jared took it all in. I watched his countenance drop. He wasn't able to hide his feelings, he tried, but it was evident that he was crushed. I've never seen an 8-year-old depressed, but Jared was. I could handle the news, but did my sweet little boy have to? He was so young. It's hard to see God work in a child's life in that way. I wanted to start screaming and just act like a baby that wasn't getting my way. For Jared's sake and everybody else's in that room, I kept a smile on my face and tried to be hopeful. Yes, I would be hopeful…for myself too.

Somehow God got us through the next couple of weeks. We had our friends and family praying for us and for our baby girl. The day we met with the cardiologist, I carried the same sinful fear, but I also held on to hope. Kyle and I went to the same office where the sonogram was done, only this time we met with a pediatric cardiologist. He was a nice man, and clearly knew what he was doing. After examining our daughter for quite some time, he told us that it appeared our daughter had heterotaxy. This is a problem that causes organs to be misplaced and is associated with heart problems and generally asplenia (no spleen) or polysplenia (many spleens). He could tell that her heart was in the right place and was not transverse (flip-flopped) as some are with this kind of problem. He could see that she only had two chambers, but it was hard to determine too much detail through a sonogram. He didn't give us terrible news though. He said she would need a few surgeries, but from what he could see, he thought they would be able to help her. He gave us hope by telling us that she could probably live a fairly normal life with the proper care. This was a tremendous encouragement to us! This sweet little daughter had problems, but there was hope. She may survive and even thrive. We praised God for this news.

Our employment and insurance issues seemed even bigger now that our baby would need a lot of medical care. We did have this cost-share, but we knew it would not be sufficient long-term, and it was still too expensive for us to keep without a good income. We continued to pray for permanent work and for good medical insurance. Shortly after the news spread about what we were facing, the vice president of the company Kyle had been contracting with offered him a full time job. This same man also worked it out so that Kyle's starting date would be the first day that he began the contract work for them. This would give us medical insurance immediately. God answered our prayers! Once again, God was showing us that our problems were not too big for him, even though they were huge to us. We couldn't even dream up a way to work it all out, but God's resources are unlimited and his abilities are great!

Chapter 7

During the next two months, I spent every morning at my kitchen table. I'd get up early so that I could be alone. I cried out to God in prayer. I searched the scriptures for help. They were the only place I could go and feel real peace and contentment. When I'm faithfully in God's word, it builds my motivation to sacrifice my all for Christ. I'm ready and willing to do anything and everything when I read about the men and women in scripture who faithfully served God. Like any other mommy would do, I asked God every day to let my little girl's problems go away. If she must have them, then I prayed that they wouldn't be severe and that she'd be able to live here with us without much intervention.

One day when I was out with my mom and my children (after both Samuel and Josiah had died), I told my mom, "I know why God didn't leave the boys here with me, because he knew that I could never handle the stress and pressure of raising a sick child." I just knew that I wasn't capable of that. I'd often heard people say, "The Bible says, God won't give me more than I can handle, and I could never handle that." That is what I used to think too, but I now know that that is not what the Bible is saying. Actually, the verse that people are referring to when they say that is I Cor. 10:13, and if you read the whole chapter, you'll see that Paul is talking about being tempted to sin. He is saying that God will never let the temptation to sin be so great that there is not a way to escape it. In other words, we can never say, "Well, there was no way to stop gossiping, yelling, fighting, fornicating, committing adultery, lusting, pouting, complaining, etc." There will always be an escape possible, and we will never be able to justify our sin.

God didn't promise that he would never give us a trial that we couldn't handle. In fact, if you look at 2 Cor. 1:8–10, you'll see quite the opposite. It says that they were "…pressed out of measure, beyond strength, despairing even of life." That doesn't sound like they were handling it. It goes on to say, "…that we should not trust in ourselves, but in God which raiseth the dead, in whom we trust that he will yet deliver us." It's not a matter of handling it ourselves; it's only through Christ that we can handle anything! And, of course, we don't have grace for a trial that we aren't in. Would anybody ever think they could handle the death of a child or a husband or wife or the loss of a limb or their eyesight? If we were to think about those things, we would never say, "Oh yeah, no problem, I could handle that." I never thought I could face the things that I've had to face, but God knew I could through his strength. It appeared God was doing now exactly what I said he wouldn't do. He knew me better than I knew myself. This is one reason why we should never try to tell God what to do for us. Sometimes we think we can dictate to God what he should do for us, making ourselves the authority and God the subordinate. Determination of self-will doesn't please God, but selfless surrender does.

I began to think about how I could have an attitude of gratefulness. If God made my little girl this way, he did it for a purpose. If she would grow up, I wanted her to grow up knowing that! She was no reject. At times I've used the accepted phrase "birth defect" for lack of a better one, but I hate that phrase. Attaching the term defect to a person just seems so dishonoring to God considering it is an insult to his creative design. One definition of the word defect is, "the lack of something necessary or desirable for completion or perfection," (American Heritage Dictionary). That's just not so with God's creations. I never thought about it until people were using that word to describe my children. I wanted our daughter to know that God made her fearfully and wonderfully, and she was not any less than any one of God's creations that was made without a physical problem. I've often said I'd much rather be Momma to a child with a health issue and a pure heart than to a child that is physically healthy and wicked. Which one would cause more grief? Without a doubt, a child that was not serving Christ would bring more sadness to me.

God was working; not only in mine and Kyle's lives but in this child's life too. This wasn't all about us. With our other babies that died, it never dawned on me that it would be their trial too, but with this baby it did, because she had a fighting chance at life. This was her life that would be affected, not just ours. God was going to be by her side as well as ours.

We began to think of names for her. God would give us this daughter's special name that he'd already chosen for her. We just needed to figure out what it was. Kyle had always let me pick names for our girls. I'm terribly old fashioned, and I love all the romantic names of the past. I loved the simple and beautiful name Anna, which means "grace." This seemed so appropriate. The description of the woman Anna, in the scriptures, was that she was a widow that was 84 years old. She served God faithfully in the temple and was blessed to see the baby Jesus before she died. (Luke 2)

For a middle name, I began searching in some name books and in our big family Bible. When I saw the name Gabriel in the back of our Bible, it said it means, "God is my strength." I knew that Gabrielle, which is a feminine version of the name, would be perfect. God's strength would carry her and help her through the challenges ahead. As I began to ponder the name, Anna Gabrielle, I just felt sure it was her name. God knew it and he had revealed it to me.

After feeling content with that task accomplished, I began my time in the scriptures. On previous days I had been reading the Psalms, but I wasn't sure what I wanted to read that morning, so I opened the Bible to begin to search for a passage. The very first passage my eyes fell upon was Isaiah 44:2. It said, "Thus saith the LORD that made thee, and formed thee from the womb, which will help thee; fear not, O (Anna), my servant." Okay, it really said "O Jacob, my servant," but I felt that God was speaking to me regarding Anna. I felt he was showing me that he formed her from the womb and would help her. I was so pleased with that little portion of scripture that I just closed my Bible, breathed a deep refreshing breath, and meditated on that little, yet big spiritual truth. Right at that moment a very distinct ray of sunshine squeezed through an opening in the mini blinds and illuminated directly on me and on my Bible. It was such a warm and comforting embrace of sunlight. I opened up my Bible again and looked down. The very first verse I looked at was Psalms 43:3: "O send out Thy light and Thy truth: let them lead me; let them bring me unto Thy holy hill, and to Thy tabernacles." Here I was receiving this beautiful stream of morning sunshine, and it was lighting itself on the verse that said, "O send out Thy light!"

I knew I was communing with God. Why wouldn't he be right there with me showing me he cared and that he loved me and was guiding me? I then flipped a few pages and my eyes landed on Isaiah 49. It said in verse 1, "The LORD hath called me from the womb; from the bowels of my mother hath he made mention of my name." Then in verse 5, "...Yet shall I be glorious in the eyes of the LORD, and my God shall be my strength." Do you remember what I said Gabrielle meant? Here I was crying out to God to give me our baby's name, and not only did he give it to me, but he used his word to verify it. The verse said,

"And God shall be my strength." That was the meaning of the name Gabrielle—God is my strength!

I must stop here and tell you that I am not a person that believes in opening up the Bible and just putting my finger on a verse and prophetically saying, "This is the verse for the day!" In fact, I'm entirely and completely put off by that type of thing. I also don't support taking verses out of context, but it wasn't like that. I was just opening up the scripture so I could search for something to read to encourage my heart and spirit, and as soon as I opened the Bible, these verses stood out like they were highlighted. My eyes didn't search for them but went directly to them upon opening the page. I really do believe that God was communicating in a special and unique way that morning. He saw my desire to seek him early. He knew how desperately I wanted and needed him at that moment.

I just sat with tears in my eyes and praised God for that special time. It truly was one of the most awesome moments of my whole life! I will never forget that morning. I was receiving a word from my precious Lord who cares about every detail of my life. I've never felt more loved by God than I did at that moment, and to think, if I hadn't been hurting and seeking God's word and help, I never would have experienced that. I was grateful that through my suffering I had this beautiful moment of inspiration and a special closeness to my Lord. I later shared every detail of my morning with Kyle. He got excited and agreed that Anna Gabrielle would definitely be our daughter's name.

Chapter 8

One specific request I made to the Lord was that Anna would spend some extra time in my womb. We were told that she would be transported by airplane to Kansas City shortly after her birth and would need surgery on her heart. I wanted her to have time to store up some extra fat reserves. I figured if she was a little plump, she would endure her trial better. I looked forward to the day she was born. I wanted to meet my precious daughter, but I wanted to do everything I could to help her to be strong. I felt that praying this way gave me something specific to *do*.

Another action step I took was that I also began to feed my family a healthy diet. I knew that if Anna was able to come home with us, it would benefit all of us if we were healthy enough to fight off sickness. The last thing Anna would need was a cold or flu on top of her heart problems. I began making whole grain bread and juicing carrots for all of us. I even made my family drink a green juice made from young barley grass twice a day. We still do all these things and more.

I was doing everything I could think of to ensure a good delivery. I was not only praying that Anna would be a little overdue, but also that I would not need an epidural. I was determined to do everything in my power to give her a great start. Sometimes having an epidural can increase the risk of other intervention, and I didn't want anything unnecessary.

My due date came and went. We waited patiently and prepared ourselves for the trial ahead. Two weeks passed my due date, I began labor. The only other time I had been overdue was with Samuel and that is very common with a baby with anencephaly, because the body produces oxytocin as the cervix is stimulated. (When the top of the skull is absent, as in the case with Samuel, it doesn't allow an abundance of stimulation to the cervix, thus not a lot of oxytocin. The result is not enough contractions to stimulate active labor.) This was my only really late baby other than him. I felt very certain that God had approved of my request and answered my prayer with a yes. It's an exciting thing to discover that your desires can truly be in accordance with God's plan.

I had my midwife checking me the day I went into labor so we wouldn't be stuck in the hospital too long before the delivery. We went to the hospital when my cervix was dilated to six or seven. We had only been there a couple of hours when I delivered Anna, and it was a great delivery. God was so merciful. I think back at what a miracle that delivery was.

I had asked God to confirm Anna's problem by her umbilical cord. When she was born, if she had a two-vessel cord, as the sonogram revealed, then that meant she did have the problems that she had been diagnosed with and if it was a normal three-vessel cord, then perhaps God had healed her. When Anna was first born, I asked my doctor if the umbilical cord was a two-vessel cord. He confirmed that it was.

Was it right to ask that of God? I'm not sure, perhaps not, but I wanted him to allow me to be immediately aware of her condition so that I wouldn't have any false hope if she was doing well.

I was a bit saddened by the news but not really surprised. I knew God could heal Anna, but it hadn't been my experience in the past to witness a complete physical healing with my children, at least not in this fashion, and I had a feeling God was doing a very special work in all of our lives and especially in Anna's.

When Anna was born, I felt like I had Abigail all over again. Not by the delivery, because there was a night and day difference in that, but because she looked so much like her big sister. She had a lot of black hair and similar features, but as I examined her more closely, I noticed differences. For one thing, Anna was a bit blue. She did pink up in time, but she definitely had a different color than my other babies. She was a big girl at eight pounds nine ounces. Nice and fat, just like I requested.

The doctors told me that with her problems there shouldn't be any immediate danger and that we could cuddle her for a while. We did and enjoyed every bit of it!

She was crying, like any new baby, and this encouraged me. I wasn't allowed to nurse her because they didn't know how soon she'd need surgery. This was difficult. I wanted to nestle her up against me and let her nurse, and she wanted to.

After about thirty minutes or more, the pediatric specialist and nurses took Anna to NICU. Kyle followed, and I went to see her as soon as I could. We didn't know when Anna would be transported to Kansas City, so my parents brought the children in to see Anna at about one o'clock in the morning. The children weren't allowed to go in and see her, so I took her up to the window and held her in front of them. We have precious pictures of them standing in front of the window trying to touch her. It warmed my heart and yet it hurt. I wondered why we were here again, a third time. I felt especially tender towards Jared and Abigail. They were old enough to grasp what was happening, and I knew it was hard for them. Cecily was too little too understand, but she and Anna were very close in age and would be great friends as Anna grew. I hoped they'd have that opportunity.

We were told that Anna would be transported to Children's Mercy hospital in Kansas City in the morning. Kyle would fly with her and the rest of us would drive. Anna would travel in a little incubator-type bed. The next morning before they left, we talked to the pediatric cardiologist that was filling in for our doctor because he was out of town. She just got right down to business. She said that Anna's heart was in terrible shape and that she would definitely need many surgeries. Then she added,

"Or there's always a heart transplant." She said it like it shouldn't affect us at all.

Didn't she realize how horrific that sounded to us? She didn't look us in the eye. She used a harsh and direct voice. She came across as cold and rude in the way she spoke. I know I was scared to death and was not dealing with any news very well, but surely she could have tried to soften the blow somehow. Something as simple as an "I'm sorry" or even a sympathetic expression would have made a big difference. I'll never understand why she chose to be a pediatric cardiologist when she seemed like a person who didn't even like children (or adults for that matter) and certainly wouldn't be able to relate to them. I know it's not right, but I must confess, I wanted to cry like a child and tell her how mean she was. Her coldness and frankness almost made me feel like I was in trouble; like I somehow caused Anna's problems. She would have made a great probation officer. It would have suited her personality better. I was beginning to wonder if there were any kind woman doctors. I knew there were, but the two I had dealt with during this trial were not.

I was released from the hospital shortly after Anna and Daddy were off. It was a fast trip for them, but I had to go home and pack up all of us and drive several hours. My mom drove me and the kids, and my dad drove separately to give us two vehicles. By the time we arrived, it had been less than twenty-four hours since I had delivered Anna. As you can imagine, I was weary physically and emotionally.

When we got to Kansas City, we couldn't find Kyle,

and we couldn't reach his cell phone. Eventually we found him at the Hyatt Regency hotel. The hospital didn't have any place for us to stay. The Ronald McDonald house couldn't keep us until the next night, and every hotel in town was booked because of a Royal's baseball game, so we had no choice but to stay in the Hyatt. It was the only hotel in town with any vacancies. It was very fancy and much too expensive for us, but we had no choice. It truly was all that was available. Jared remembers how cool he thought it was to stay so high up and in such a nice hotel. I guess God picked that hotel just for him, because the cost stressed us out, but the experience thrilled him!

I remember waking up that first morning feeling guilty that Anna had spent the night alone in the hospital. She needed me, and I needed to get to her as soon as possible. I felt somewhat desperate. After roaming the halls of Children's Mercy Hospital and trying to find our way, we finally made it to where Anna was. Doctors were there giving us confusing information. It was all so new and foreign to us. I remember as they were doing a sonogram of her abdomen, they showed us her uterus. They were just telling us what it was they were looking at. The emotions in my heart were very strange. I found myself wondering if God would ever place a child in her womb or if it would always remain empty. Anna's future was just so uncertain. While doing the sonogram, they also told us that Anna had asplenia. This made her diagnosis a bit worse than if she had had polysplenia. Asplenia meant no spleen function at all, because there was no spleen. I knew that this would compromise her immune system even more. I hated receiving the news. As the tests continued, the results just kept getting worse.

Anna's heart problems were very complex. She had a single ventricle, tapvr (total anomalous pulmonary venous return), coarctation of the aorta, double outlet right ventricle, and many other things associated with this. Her liver was mid-line, and her stomach was also on the right side instead of the left, but this didn't pose any problems. They were both functioning just fine. The first step was to do what was called a closed heart surgery. They would go in between two bones of her rib cage and put a band on her pulmonary artery and fix the coarctation of the aorta. They expected her to do well.

Our family stayed at the Ronald McDonald house during the rest of our stay in Kansas City. It was a blessing to have somewhere to stay that didn't require us to pay more than we could. It is a great ministry for families in need. We did have a few "clown house" (as Kyle calls it) trials. We almost got kicked out because my mom had just recovered from a severe case of pneumonia and was still coughing. She was not contagious, but somebody turned us in and said that they were scared for the safety of their sick child with a sick woman in the house, which of course is understandable. A nurse stuck up for us and told the house manager that pneumonia can create a cough that can stick around for months (and it had). So, we didn't have to leave. Cecily, our two-year-old who was full of energy, got us in trouble a time or two. I don't think they were accustomed to housing seven people for one patient. My parents would stay with the children during the day while Kyle and I were at the hospital. We'd come back at night to sleep.

There were seven of us in one room with two full beds. The children slept on the floor. It was pretty loud at night hearing two men snore in one little room. I felt like we were housing grizzly bears! The only reason we could sleep in the midst of all that snoring was because we were all exhausted!

It was tight quarters and somewhat stressful at times, but it was nice to be together, snoring and all! I am so grateful for my parents' willingness to give up their own lives for us for nearly two weeks. The children, and Grandma and Grandpa, were all able to go in and see Anna a few times. They loved seeing her and holding her. They were bonding with their little sissy and granddaughter.

The first five days Anna was being fed through her veins instead of her stomach. She would be able to eat after she had recovered enough from the surgery. I was pumping breast milk every four hours to keep up my milk supply, so when we were able to leave I would be able to nurse Anna.

She had the surgery when she was three days old and it went very well. There weren't any problems at all. By the time we got to see her, she was off the ventilator and breathing well on her own. She began drinking breast milk from a bottle when she was six days old and took it well. I was able to begin nursing her on her eighth day, and we were heading home when Anna was ten days old. We were excited to get home and enjoy some normalcy, even if it would be a new normal.

Chapter 9

It felt so good to be home! Anna had gotten pretty skinny through her ordeal, but she was nursing well, so I expected her to plump up quickly. I am so glad she started off with those extra reserves of fat! God was good to provide that for Anna. When we had been home for nearly a month, we had to make one trip back to the hospital for just a couple of days because Anna's pediatric cardiologist noticed from an x-ray that she had some fluid around her heart. It wasn't uncommon for that to happen after heart surgery, but we didn't know that at the time, so it did scare us. They put her on a heavy dose of Lasix for a couple days and sent us back home.

We were home and would settle in to some sort of routine. Well, maybe not just yet. A sensible couple would have done just that, but not Kyle and I. We had a desire to live out in the country. We wanted to live somewhere where Anna, when old enough, could play outside in the fresh air (if there's any left in the world). We knew that neighborhood children posed a risk for Anna. If any of the children got sick, they would bring it home to Anna. Before we left the hospital, the nurses told us to try very hard to keep her healthy. We were told that a simple cold could be dangerous for Anna, especially while she was a baby. Country living seemed like the perfect solution. It had been our dream, and even though I just wanted to enjoy my new baby, I also wanted to get to the country to protect her.

We found an old farm house on ten acres. Our house sold very quickly, so there was no turning back. The new house was a dump, but Kyle had plans for it. We moved in before we closed on the house. We even put some carpet in and had some other work done. For some reason, the termite inspection was left until the last minute. When it was done, the inspector told us that the house trusses were completely eaten through by termites. This house needed about $40,000 worth of repair! We were already spending more than we really should have and would need to spend more to fix it up. The owners were not able to spend that money to fix it, so in the end, we had to move out. The move to the house had been so difficult with four children and one of them being a new baby that needed extra care. I didn't think I'd survive another move. However, we found a house that we loved immediately. It was a hundred years old but in much better shape structurally than the other one. It was on five acres.

This house was nearly an hour's drive from the other one and about forty-five minutes drive from my family and our church. I always liked living close to my parents. I never would have supported this move before, but I just wanted out of what we'd nicknamed the Nightmare House. Not only did it have major termite damage, but there were animals scratching on the floor from underneath the house and snakes were all over the yard. It truly was like a nightmare! Kyle had always wanted to live up north a ways (north of Wichita), and God knew it would take being desperate and homeless to get me there!

We've really enjoyed this old farm! We raised seventy-five chicks in our basement for about three weeks. (It stunk to high heaven in the house, and we'll never do that again!) We milked goats, (Jared even rode one like a horse for about two seconds). We carelessly bred way too many kittens (as many as twenty-seven at one time!) We butchered chickens. We enjoyed many campfires. We raised guineas (but the dog liked them too much), and we even tried to keep sheep but that was not a good experience. When the sheep would get out, Kyle would chase them down with his dirt bike. It didn't work very well, but he had a great time trying! We've had a lot of fun out here. This house, being so old, has been expensive and a lot of work. We didn't realize what we were getting into when we moved here, but maybe someday it will be just the way we want it, and if not, we'll just continue to enjoy it the way it is. As Anne Shirley said of Diana Barry's rich aunt, in the movie Anne of Green Gables, "No wonder she has so little imagination. That's one consolation of being poor; you have to dream all this up!" Imagination is a wonderful tool for creativity, and we've had to use it a lot!

Chapter 10

When Anna was nine months old, she needed her first open-heart surgery. I dreaded that day, but I knew that she needed it, and I just wanted it over with. My parents, always willing to step in and help, came to stay with our kiddos. We didn't know how long we would be away. We had a farm to work, goats to milk, chickens to feed, and eggs to collect. Jared and Abigail were only 8 ½ and not quite 6 years old. While we were gone, they did all the chores, including the milking twice a day. Grandpa kept them goin,' and Grandma strained the milk and served big glasses of goat milk with every meal. She was afraid of wasting it so she served regular milk, chocolate milk, and pudding—anything with milk! I told her later that she could have just thrown it out or given it to the cats, but she was determined not to waste any of it.

The night before Anna's surgery we were staying in a hotel. Anna woke up to nurse. The pre-surgery paper included the instruction that I could only give Anna clear liquids after two o'clock a.m., and they said that breast milk wasn't a clear liquid. So, even though she had never had anything but breast milk and hadn't ever used a bottle beyond those first few days in the hospital, I was going to attempt to give her some room temperature apple juice. We had practiced ahead of time to get her used to the bottle, but it didn't work. She hated it. To my surprise, at 1:30 a.m., she actually drank about half of the apple juice before she realized it wasn't what she was used to. I was able to just snuggle her after that and she went back to sleep. I had been really stressed about that part of it, and I was so happy that God gave her contentment with that apple juice.

When we got her to the hospital, we had to hand her over to the nurse so they could prepare her for surgery. A nine-month-old child knows Mommy and Daddy well. She did not want to leave. We told her we loved her and gave her kisses and then sent her down the hall with the nurse. She cried the whole way down the hall, and so did we. Kyle and I were scared. This was a major surgery. Would Anna come through it okay? We knew it was very risky.

It took many hours. A nurse named Beth would come and update us about every twenty to thirty minutes. She would tell us everything that was going on. Every time she came out, she had a good report. We were so relieved. Kyle spent the time reading. I spent the time writing in my journal. I guess writing has always been a release for me. We couldn't wait until it was all over and we were back at home again.

After what seemed like an eternity, Beth came out and

told us that they were closing her up and that everything went well. She said that they had taken her off of the heart/lung machine and would be taking the ventilator out soon. When she came back about ten minutes later, she said, "Anna got very sick." We were shocked. Just a short time before, she had been doing well. What could have gone so wrong? She said that when they took the ventilator out, Anna's heart stopped. They had to do chest compressions and force oxygen into her lungs. When her heart started beating again, they put the ventilator back in. Her vitals were not good.

They weren't sure what happened. They said they'd have to wait until she was stable before they could attempt to discover the problem. We were able to see Anna after about half an hour. I think they wanted to give us time with her as soon as they could, because they told us there was a good chance she wouldn't pull through.

It broke my heart to see her hooked up to so many machines. It was all very familiar. When Josiah was sick, he looked very much the same…so little compared to all the big machines. The beeps and other noises were familiar too. Bad dreams of those noisy machines had haunted my sleep many nights after Josiah died, and now I was hearing them again with Anna hooked up to them instead of Josiah. I wanted Anna to be okay. I wanted her to be able to go home. I hated every moment of this! I talked to Anna and told her I loved her, but she was on so much medication she couldn't respond. We both kept talking to her though. Kyle and I prayed for her and talked to her about Jesus. We kept telling her that we were there and that Jesus was too. While in NICU, we would often play the Anne of Green Gables video or listen to pretty music: anything to remind her (and us) of home.

Day after day, there was no improvement. We hoped the numbers on the machines would show her body was making positive changes, but they didn't. Anna's vitals were not good at all. She was still too unstable for even a heart catheterization to determine what was wrong. So, we waited.

I remember going into a room to pump breast milk, and I would use that time to cry out to the Lord. I would just sob and pray in one desperate word, "Please, please, please." No other words would come. I was too weak. I was desperate, but I knew that I needed to pray. I was so scared to lose her. I had watched my two babies die, but I didn't know them like I knew Anna. This was my little girl who I had nursed, cared for, and loved for nine months. I couldn't live without her.

We never had any good news to give when we would call home to talk to the children. I knew they were getting discouraged too. We missed the other three children so much. It had been nearly nine days and nothing had changed. I worried about how long we were going to be stuck at Children's Mercy Hospital. I had heard stories about children being in the hospital for months after heart surgery. How would we do it if it came to that? We lived several hours away from Kansas City. Kyle would have to go back to work at some point. I prayed God would spare us a long stay.

On day nine, they decided to do another heart cath. Anna really wasn't any more stable, but she wasn't improving at all, and they needed to try to help her. When the heart cath was done, and the results were in, they told us that they discovered Anna had an obstruction in her veins. During her first surgery, they had done the hemi-fontan and had also repaired the tapvr. When they repaired those things, it actually created this obstruction, so they needed to go back in to fix this. They would do the surgery the next day. I was relieved to know that there was something they could repair. It would have been bad news if they wouldn't have found anything physically wrong. There was a reason she wasn't getting better.

When she went in for this surgery, we knew it was her only hope. We knew this surgery would either fix her or she would die. I read my Bible during the wait. I prayed, and I wrote in my journal. Kyle and I didn't talk much. We both just kind of kept to ourselves. It was hard to know what to talk about. Both of our minds were filled with only one thing—taking Anna home. Some of the time we just stared at a television screen in the waiting room, not really seeing or hearing anything.

After several hours, the doctor walked in, and we practically ran to him. He had a pleasant look on his face. In fact it was almost a smile, so we were encouraged. He sat us back down and told us that he had fixed the obstruction and that Anna was doing well. He really thought that Anna would be all right. Hallelujah! You talk about feeling like letting out a "whoop," well that's what we felt like. We may have even done it! We were so relieved and grateful! We praised God and then called the family to give them the first good news in ten days!

We continued to wait in the waiting room until she was transferred back to NICU. Only now we were rejoicing, because we knew that there was a reason Anna wasn't getting better, and her problem was now fixed. It didn't take long and we were able to go and be with her. They didn't attempt to take the ventilator out because of her last experience, so she was still hooked up to everything, but I was just so happy she was alive and that there was hope.

As Anna was recovering, she began to respond to us. She didn't feel well, that was obvious by her fussing and crying, but she knew we were there and tried to reach out to us. Had we not just endured the two weeks that we had, it would have been unbearable to see that look in her eyes and watch her suffer as she became more aware of her pain. It did break my heart to watch my little girl cry and look so miserable, but I was also rejoicing because she was reaching out and attempting to communicate with us. That could only mean she was getting better.

When she was well enough for us to hold her, I did as often as they'd let me. When I would hold Anna, her oxygen saturation level would go up. The machines numbers revealed how her body responded to my embrace. She also did this when Daddy held her and talked to her. The first time I was able to nestle her next to me and nurse her was pure joy! She and I both loved it, and I know Daddy was blessed by the sweet reunion as well. His little girl was getting better. In the following days she just got better and better and miraculously, ten days after her second surgery, we were on our way home! It had been three weeks since we had seen our other children. We were so excited and so were they. We all missed each other so much! When we got home, we hugged and hugged and just enjoyed each other. All the children looked different to me. We were used to being together every single day. It was very strange to be away from them for three weeks.

It took some time, but Anna did recover from that horrible ordeal. We had to wean her off of narcotic drugs (which was terrible!), and it took time for her to regain her strength, but we had made it down a very rough road, and we were so grateful to God for sparing her life. Life would be a little sweeter.

Chapter 11

I can't even begin to express the joy that was in my heart during the holidays that year. I read the Christmas story over and over and just felt an overwhelming love for Jesus. I was so happy, so content, and so very grateful for my life and for my sweet relationship with Kyle and our four precious children that God placed in our care. As I think back, I marvel. I had watched two of my children die. I had watched my little girl barely hang on to life, but I was happier and more content than I had ever been. That's a miracle! What wonderful evidence of a loving Savior and the peace and comfort only he can give. It brings to life I Peter 12: 13–14: "Beloved, think it not strange concerning the fiery trial which is to try you as though some strange thing happened unto you: But rejoice, inasmuch as ye are partakers of Christ's sufferings; that, when his glory shall be revealed, ye may be glad also with exceeding joy." The trial had brought gladness and I was exceedingly joyful!

I wouldn't recommend being away from your children to test this theory, but it is true that absence makes the heart grow fonder. I missed my precious little ones so much, I almost couldn't stand it. When I had daily access to them again, I loved every minute of it! Even the things that moms would consider *trying* brought me joy. I was just happy to be home working through the events of the day.

Because Anna was still so fragile, we still had to be very careful with her. Through the fall and winter months when colds and the flu run rampant, we all stayed home. Well, all except for Kyle. He, of course, had to go to work, but he also ran errands and bought groceries and such. I was nursing and caring for Anna, so I needed to be extra careful. On a rare occasion we would go somewhere together, but usually it was just a drive, or we'd go through a drive-thru and get something to eat (which was also slightly risky having someone that may be sick prepare and handle our food).

It was a bit lonely at times. We had moved so far away from everything and everyone we knew. We couldn't take Anna to church and didn't want to be divided for worship, so we sang together and learned from Kyle during the cold months. We knew the day would come when we could get back into a fellowship with other Christians. It was just a few months and spring and summer would be here.

Protecting Anna was worth it, but it was a whole new life. We leaned on each other and on the Lord! I remember crying to my mom on more than one occasion, telling her how much I missed my family and friends. I needed people in my life more than I realized, but I was learning to be content in my unique situation. It was a bit of a weaning for me as well. I will always need and love my mom, but I learned to depend more on Kyle as I didn't have access to my mom all the time. Kyle learned to be more helpful as well, as I think he depended a great deal on my mom too!

We learned some very valuable lessons during this time in our lives. We began to discover more about ourselves and our personal walks with the Lord. It's so easy when you attend church to try to measure up. We realized that we did things, not because we felt that's what God wanted us to do, but because that's what was expected of us. We were forced to be free from that, thus we were free to discover what God wanted for us. If we all loved the Lord perfectly and we were humble and selfless, we wouldn't need times like these, but this turned out to be a good thing for our family. We realized we had been doing some performing and needed to back away and discover who we really were and what our motivation was.

Some of our so-called walk with the Lord had been a mere performance. We also found that in our conversation, our hearts had been judgmental. If people weren't doing the things we did, we assumed they weren't as close to the Lord as we were. We truly did love the Lord: He'd delivered us from our lost state. He had shown us love when we didn't deserve it. He had brought us through some terribly hard times. Yes, we loved Jesus, but we also loved the praise of men. We wanted people to like us and approve of the things we were doing. It almost became a spiritual competition.

This was also an awesome time to learn about our freedom in Christ! How many traditions do we cling to for the sake of acceptance? How many people do we reject or turn away because they don't follow our traditions?

Do we judge people according to their church attendance or how many church activities they've signed up for? Do we make a phone call to someone that wasn't in church to see if there is something we can help them with, or do we just call to see if they skipped out on church for no good reason so that we can have one-up on them or gossip about them?

There were times that I missed a church service because I or a family member was ill, and then I'd feel disappointment. Not because I missed out on the preaching, or the worship, or the fellowship with other Christians, but because somebody who might be keeping track of attendance might not be impressed! I found that I was more concerned with man's opinions of me than God's.

I remember missing several weeks in a row one time because two of our children had whooping cough (or something like it), and I asked a mature friend if she thought people would look down on us for missing so many services. She said, "Lynnette, you shouldn't concern yourselves with what others think but only with what God thinks." As long as you are pleasing the Lord, man's opinions mean nothing." I was so insecure when I was young in the Lord. I found myself saying and doing things that I knew would impress my brothers and sisters in Christ instead of saying and doing things to please

Christ. As the years have gone by, it has gotten easier to focus on pleasing God and not man. I've realized that if I'm truly pleasing my Lord, man doesn't have any valid reason to be at odds with me.

It is important to be with God's people. We should prioritize our time with other Christians. We should look forward to being nourished by God's word through preaching. We should love encouraging others in Christ. We should love to go and worship together with other believers through our prayers and song. We should want to be there for those reasons, not to impress people. The verse that's often used by the preacher/teacher to encourage faithful attendance is "not forsaking the assembling of yourselves together..." Hebrews 10:25, but the word *forsake* means "to abandon" or "leave entirely." Missing a service on occasion doesn't mean that you are abandoning the church.

So many churches focus more on church attendance than they do on loving Christ. Sick people come to church to share their germs with others. Is that love? New moms bring their one or two-day-old infant to church so that she can beat the record on how soon a new mom can get to church after her baby is born! I've actually seen this happen and have even participated in the game!

Why do we focus so much on man's opinions of us? It just doesn't make sense. If you step away from the church for a time (a short time), you may realize that you have more freedom than you think. Not freedom to skip church for no reason or to slack off in your Bible-reading, but freedom to think outside the box, freedom to worship together as a family and give up some of the activities. You can be so involved in activities that your family isn't even going to church together.

When we were forced to stay home for a time, we were free from the abundance of organized ministries. Families are so busy ministering at church that they are falling apart. There are youth ministries, ladies Bible studies, men's Bible studies, junior churches, nurseries, young married groups...old married...unmarried....used to be married, and on and on. Sign on the dotted line.... the more times you sign, the more highly esteemed you are, but in whose eyes? Is Christ pleased? Are we truly seeking to minister, or are we just enjoying getting involved. What does it mean to truly minister?

I recently heard a story of a young mother with multiple sclerosis. She had just given birth to her fourth child. Her oldest child was only five years old. She was staying with her parents during this time because her family had recently moved out of state and didn't want to deliver the baby there. An acquaintance of this new mother contacted a lady from her mother's church to see if they might want to provide a few meals for them. She was told that since the daughter and her family weren't members of the church, they wouldn't be able to provide meals. This was a missed opportunity. I know that our Lord would not be pleased with that.

What is church ministry? It is when the body of Christ, no matter what local church you attend, ministers to others in need. Galatians 6:10: "As we have therefore opportunity, let us do good unto all men, especially unto them who are of the household of faith." Notice it doesn't say especially unto those of your local church assembly, but those of the household of faith. We are to reach out to all men, but especially Christians in need. Start at home and work up to more from there as you are able to.

While it's not wrong to be a servant of Christ and, in fact, is right to be, it is wrong to serve in the wrong way. It's wrong to neglect your God-given duty of being a faithful wife standing beside your husband. It's wrong to neglect being a faithful husband caring for and loving your wife by taking care of her and meeting her physical and emotional needs. It's wrong to neglect being a protective and nurturing parent. It's so easy to give that job to the Sunday school teacher or the youth group leader. How many parents give the job to them?

Our family enjoyed serving in ways that we could. We served each other at home. We sang worship songs together, which ministered to each other and blessed the Lord. We reached out to others that God put in our path....somehow (even though we were homebodies). Kyle helped a lady on the road with her broken-down vehicle one day. While helping her he found out that she was a young widow with several young children. He came home and told me about her. We felt that God had put her in his path so that we could have a ministry and touch her life. It was as much for us as for her. I made some homemade bread and some other goodies for her, and we gave her a little bit of money. We didn't have much to give, but we gave what we could. We told her about a church that we knew of in the area and we told her to call us if she had more needs. She wasn't a Christian, but we did it all in the name of the Lord Jesus Christ, and felt great about it!

I know that we are to do our alms (good deeds) before God and not men. I only mention this as an example to show that even in our loneliness, away from every organized ministry, God gave us one! In fact, he gave us other opportunities to minister too. We were able to give Christmas gifts to a family who had lost their husband/father. We were able to take food to a local charity, but we felt our most important ministry for others was prayer. This was something we could do together as a family. We didn't have to go anywhere to do it and yet we knew that God wanted us to pray fervently for others.

Often we are so busy running to church (or a church meeting) that we forget to slow down and see what is going on around us. How often do we drive past a broken down widow on our way to church choir? Our work for Christ goes way beyond the four church walls! In fact, I would venture to say, it starts within the four walls of our home and extends out from there. God gave us an every day ministry in our children. He gave us a child with special needs as well. It's so easy to forget that our ministry inside the home is our first and most important ministry.

As Fraulein Maria said, "When the Lord closes a door, somewhere he opens a window." Even though we were stuck in the house and somewhat lonely for our loved ones, we spent some really precious time together. The kids and I would take a break in the middle of school for a tea party. We read the whole *Little House on the Prairie* series. We picked dandelions and learned to make dandelion jelly. We also dipped them in batter and fried them. This is now a favorite spring treat! We took time for things that were just plain fun and frivolous.

Anna, being the baby of the family, was our entertainment. We would make her laugh, teach her to do cute little tricks, and eventually teach her to walk. Because her surgery was at nine months, this set her back, and she didn't try to walk until she was about seventeen months old. She could get around just fine though. She would sit down with her legs loosely crossed and put her hands between her legs and scoot on her bottom. She didn't crawl. This was her way of getting around the house. It was adorable. One time I caught her playing with the stereo. She was about eighteen months old. She had her back to me. She had turned the dial to a hard rock station and was swaying back and forth (her way of dancing). I took the video camera and said, "Anna, what *are* you listening to?" She turned it off *real* quick and turned around like she wasn't guilty at all. It was so funny.

It was about this time that Kyle fell with Anna and landed on her leg. He was holding her in one arm and had a Coke in the other. We had a phone cord placed carelessly across the floor for internet access, and he tripped over it. Bless his heart, he was in denial, but I knew that something was terribly wrong. She would try to stand up and would immediately drop to the floor. As you can imagine, he felt horrible. Still to this day, he has a hard time talking about it. She was in a full leg cast. It was bright pink! She managed to get around quite well in it.

Because Anna was sedentary until she was nearly two, she would sit and listen and just take everything in. I think it's because of this that she learned to talk at a very young age. One time when she was barely two years old, we went to a friend's house for a Christmas party. When we got out of the car, I didn't realize that Anna was still buckled in (usually Jared or Abigail would unbuckle her and she would get herself out). I said, "Come on Anna, what's taking you so long?" she then said, "I can't get dis cuntwapchun to work," as she was trying to undo the car seat buckle! We laughed all night about that one!

When we were at the grocery store one time, Anna was talking to me in the check-out line. A little boy who was waiting in line behind us kind of gasped and loudly said, "She can talk!" She was so little and had such a big vocabulary, it was funny. Another friend said she was like a cartoon character, because it just seemed so unreal that such big words came out of such a little person.

Chapter 12

When Anna was a baby, I feared getting pregnant. I feel ashamed to admit it. Would I ever learn to truly trust God? I didn't so much fear having another baby with a problem. What I worried about was the possibility of not being able to be with Anna. I wondered what I would do if I was due to have a baby and Anna suddenly needed medical care of some kind, and I couldn't be with her. What if I was nursing my baby and she needed her surgery, and I had to leave my baby behind at home or take my baby and not be able to be with Anna through everything? I constantly worried, but none of those things ever came to pass.

I gained experience in this area. I learned that almost everything I worried about never happened. For instance, when we found out that Anna had to go back to the hospital after her first surgery it was because her x-ray showed fluid around her heart. Because of that x-ray, I found myself worrying about every x-ray! When we would get her chest x-ray before her check-ups at the cardiologist, I would always try to get information out of the technician, and when they wouldn't tell me anything, I would assume something didn't look right. I did this every single time we went to her cardiology appointments.

Worrying is a sickness. It feels like a sickness and it affects your mind and body like a sickness. I hate it. The only cure for worry is resting in Jesus, truly resting. I love the verse, "Be anxious for nothing, but in everything by prayer and supplication with thanksgiving, let your request be made known unto God, and the peace of God which passeth all understanding shall keep your hearts and minds through Christ Jesus," (Phil. 4:6–7).

Prayer really is the key to conquering worry, but what good is prayer if we forget that God is in control? Praying and knowing that whatever comes to pass is God's will is so important. There is also a third element, at least for me, and that is making the decision to trust. It goes back to what I said previously about realizing that God's plan is what it is. As much as I may not want what he has planned, it is crucial that I remember that it is God who has called me to it, and he has a plan to bring good from it.

Of course our prayers are all worked into it somehow, but "The steps of a good man are ordered by the Lord." I believe that there are times that God answers my prayers according to my desires, but is it possible that I just happened to pray for what he already had planned? I think of Psalm 37:4 that says, "Delight thyself also in the LORD, and he shall give thee the desires of thine heart."

Perhaps I can pray more appropriately if I delight in him. There are times God says no, and leads me down another path. Sometimes that path leads to something that is obviously better and sometimes that path leads to pain that is ultimately better, even if I have trouble seeing it at the time.

It takes work when it comes to walking with the Lord and trusting him. It is not an easy walk. Resting in Jesus doesn't just happen. I can quench the Spirit or I can live in the Spirit. When I feel my mind and heart getting weak, I have to go to God's word, and seek him in prayer. It's important for me to remind myself of what I already know about God. I have to pray and ask the Lord to give me peace. Then I have to walk away allowing not only my mind but also my heart to absorb the truth and hang onto it. Declaring God's goodness gives me strength and reflecting on what God has done gives me courage. One verse that I love is Psalm 73:28. It says, "It is good for me to draw near to God. I have put my trust in the LORD God, that I may declare all Thy works."

Sometimes when I feel that Kyle is wrong about something or has let me down in some way, I can reverse my feelings if I reflect on his past acts of love and kindness. It takes work to pull my mind away from those negative thoughts. It's much like that in my relationship with the Lord. If I begin to feel that he is requiring too much of me or I just feel hopeless, fearful, and discouraged, then I purpose to take time to consciously reflect on his love for me and his wonderful works in my life. In doing this, I'm putting on a new set of eyes. These eyes aren't focused on me but on him. It takes real effort, but it works, and it's even easier to do with God, because he's never let me down and has never been wrong.

When Anna was a little over two-years-old, the pregnancy that I feared happened. Only when it happened, I wasn't fearful, I was excited. God took fear away from me and gave me joy unspeakable! Once again, I had worried unnecessarily. I really was looking forward to another little one. The only sad part was that I needed to stop nursing Anna. She was a toddler, so she would get along just fine without it, but I would miss that time with her and I knew she'd miss it too. Nursing was something I did to nourish her, of course, but it also nourished me in a different way. It was precious time spent with my sweet daughter.

This would be baby number seven! When I had had five and even six children, people would say, "Wow! You look too young to have had that many children!" But when I was pregnant with number seven, people would just say, "Oh, how nice." I wondered if I was starting to look old. It must have been the stress I'd endured! I'm convinced that stress ages a person. Shortly after Samuel died, and I was not yet twenty-four, my little sister found my first gray hair and proclaimed to everybody in the room that she'd done so. I said, "It's well deserved. It's been a tough year!"

I was sicker with this baby than I had been with any of them. It was terrible. I craved strange things, as usual, but

I couldn't keep most of it down. I ran the kids to the mall (thirty minutes away) one morning just so that I could get a big pretzel with cheese. I ate a sub sandwich for breakfast one day too! Both things sounded so good but tasted horrible and made me sick. Isn't pregnancy great? It wasn't too long though and I began to feel better.

It was a blessed day when Silas John came into the world! He was another "chicken baby," like Cecily had been. I was scared and chickened out of a natural birth, so I had an epidural. Besides the epidural not working well and having to be re-done three times, it was a good delivery.

It was fun having a boy again! It had been eleven years since I'd been left with a little boy to bring up! I had had four boys and three girls, but since two of the boys had died, it had been a girl-heavy family for a while. Now, instead of one boy and three girls, we would have two boys and three girls. Nearly eleven years later, Jared finally had a brother to enjoy!

We all had such fun! The only problem was that everybody wanted to hold Silas. There were six of us trying to hog him. We had a hard time taking turns. Anna loved holding him and staring at him, but she was a bit jealous too. She had been the baby for almost three years and had nursed for over two years. With that keen little brain of hers, she hadn't forgotten those days of nursing, and when she saw Silas taking over in that department, she cried and said, "Mommy, I nurse." My dad teased her, but I felt sorry for her. I probably would have given in and nursed her too, but she got over it rather quickly, so I let it go. I think she just wanted me. She had been my baby for so long, and she wasn't sure she wanted to share me.

Silas was such a laid-back baby. He would put his arms behind his head when he slept. He was very mellow until he was about two years old. He hit two, and he hit hyper! He walked on his toes and jumped and ran as often as he could. He's really great entertainment! He's always making us laugh.

When Silas was two years old, another little brother joined our family. Jonas Quinn was baby number eight, and he was healthy! It was our first even numbered baby that wasn't born with a problem! We praised God, not because we wouldn't have adored another baby with health issues, but because God had spared us any more trials of this nature for the time being. If God would have put us in that situation again, we would have been up to the task, but since he didn't, we decided we weren't!

I had never been blessed with two boys in a row that lived. I was a little fearful about this combination! No, not really, but I was expecting it to be a bit more of a challenge. Jared and Abigail had always been fairly mature for their ages and had gotten along very well and played well together. Cecily and Anna had a great time doing girly things and never got into much trouble, but what was it going to be like having two boys just two years apart? Time would tell.

I have journals filled up with all the funny things my kiddos have said and done. I like to go back and just laugh at them. One time, on her fifth birthday, at 6:45 a.m., Anna said, "Mommy, I'm five years old today. I brushed my teeth, brushed my hair, got dressed, folded my jammies, and put them away." Later on that day, she was helping me scrub the floor. While she was scrubbing she said, "I'll miss being four, it was fun, but I like being a big girl." Another journaled event was about Cecily. When she was about five years old she said that she was going to name her husband, "Monzo" (actually Laura Ingalls' husband *Almonzo*). We tried to explain to her that she wouldn't be able to name her husband, but she couldn't quite understand.

Cecily and Anna became the best of friends. They did everything together! They loved to play dress up, and they enjoyed acting out the roles of Laura and Mary from *Little House on the Prairie*. They colored and sang, had tea parties, danced, and just did all the things little girls love to do together.

Jared and Abigail enjoyed making movies together. They had their own little special moments, like putting a radio drama or audio book on while they drank hot chocolate and did a huge puzzle (that they never finished). They've had fun creating their own audio books and radio dramas too. Jared had a way of convincing Abigail to do some pretty adventurous things! He's had her in our tree row (called the "forest") building tree branch forts, hunting rabbits, and playing Robin Hood. She never could get him to play dolls! That's probably a good thing.

It's so wonderful to have memories that make you smile! I often stop and do the frivolous things, just to make a memory! I picture myself, someday, sitting down and listening to my grown children talk about their childhood. I imagine them saying, *Remember when Mom would make chocolate chip tea scones, and we'd have a tea party? Remember when Mom would dance with us in the kitchen? Remember all the times we went to the zoo and howled at the wolves to try to get them to howl back? Remember how we'd walk by the Kookabura Canteen at the zoo and Mom always made us sing, 'Kookabura sits in the old gum tree. Merry merry king of the bush is he. Laugh! Kookaburra laugh! Kookaburra, gay your life must be.' Remember how we used to sit and watch Little House on the Prairie every day at two until we had seen each one at least ten times? Remember how Mom used to cry at every show? Remember how Mom would try to use different accents when reading books or doing devotion and she'd always sound Chinese?*

What I don't want to hear is *Mom was always too busy. Mom never sat down and did anything with us. Mom gritted her teeth all of the time or yelled when we irritated her.* All moms have bad days. All moms sin. But if there are enough great times, those are what the children will remember! Who wants to reflect on the bad times when there are so many fun times to talk about? Memories are worth taking time to make!

Chapter 13

When Anna was about three years old, she went in for a scheduled heart catheterization. She had already had phase one of the Fontan procedure, but she still needed phase two. The heart cath would determine whether she was ready for it. In order for this surgery to be successful, she needed to have the right pressure in her veins and other factors had to be just right.

After the heart cath, the pediatric cardiologist sat us down in a meeting room that was set up with long tables and chairs. This was where the doctors would meet to discuss patient's cases. The lights went off, and before us, on a large screen, was a video of Anna's heart. We'd been in this room many times before and had never received any good news. We hoped that this time would be different. We had prayed that God was improving Anna's heart.

As Dr. Kaine talked and showed us valves, veins, etc., we tried to get an idea of what it was he was saying. This doctor was one with a warm heart. He never said anything roughly or without feeling. He was perfect for this job. We praised God for him. After some hesitation, at last he said with tenderness and a slight shake of his head, "Guys, I just don't think Anna would do well with this surgery right now. It's great that she is doing so well. To be honest, I never expected that. At some point, she may be ready, I'm not losing hope, but I think the surgery would do her more harm than good." He proceeded to tell us that he would consult with the other doctors and Dr. Lofland, the surgeon, to make sure they agreed, but he expected them to say the same thing.

I had mixed emotions. My first thought was, *I just wish we could get it over with.* I really just wanted all the surgeries done so I wouldn't have to think about them anymore. On the other hand, she didn't have to have another open heart surgery yet, and I felt somewhat relieved about that.

She was older now and knew more of what was going on. When she had to have this heart cath, it was heart-breaking to witness her fear. She had a lot of inner strength and was working through it, but she, like any of us would be, wasn't happy about this medical procedure. When we were on our way to Kansas City for that particular heart cath, Anna was a little quiet and seemed to be deep in thought, but she held her thoughts in until we were about an hour away and then she belted out, "I don't want to go! Please take me home." I turned away from her to fight back the tears. I asked God for strength so that I could encourage her. I got myself together and then turned to her and said, "We have no choice honey. I don't want you to have to go either, but it is something that we all have to go through with. Now be strong. God will give you strength, and we will be on our way back home tomorrow." She still wasn't happy, but she did calm down. She knew no matter how hard she tried, she would not be able to get out of it.

Anna always had the ability to trust us, which blessed our hearts. I didn't want her to have to go through any of this either, but love endures all things. Since Anna couldn't have the surgery, I just praised God that she didn't have to go through the pain and fear of it all, and I praised God that we didn't have to watch her go through it.

Besides some horrible migraines, Anna did very well. She always tired easier than the other children, but for the most part did everything that the other children did. She learned to read quickly. She loved to sing and play piano. She was a social butterfly and enjoyed people (people enjoyed her too). When she hadn't had enough social time, I'd find her sitting in the pantry talking to herself. She would use her hands when she talked. I loved to peek in without her seeing me and just listen to her great imagination at work!

When it was nap time, I'd lie down with the girls. I'd read a book to them and then stay there until they'd fall asleep. Kyle started this little game with Anna. He'd say, "Hey, Anna!" She'd say, "What?" And then he'd say, "Go to sleep!" She'd say, "Okay." Then he'd say, "Hey, Anna!" She'd say, "What?" And he'd say again, "Go to sleep!" This would go on and on! I also had a game I'd play with Anna. We called it The Smile Game. We'd both close our eyes, and then one of us would open our eyes really wide and smile really big! We could hear each other's lips make the smile noise, and so we'd open up our eyes and smile back. It was a huge, silly smile. We'd do it over and over and eventually start cracking up. Once we got started we couldn't quit! It wasn't a very smart nap time activity, because it's hard to get tired after laughing, but we'd eventually quit and she'd roll over and go to sleep.

One special memory I have is Anna coming down with me at 6:30 in the morning to read the Bible. She was an early bird. On cold mornings we would sit in hers and Cecily's little Looney Tunes chairs and put our feet on the heater vent. We would drink our coffee (Decaf French Vanilla for Anna) and read our Bibles. This was before she could read, so I would read to her. Sometimes she would sit with her Bible on her lap and pretend she was reading it.

With Anna doing well and no surgery scheduled anytime in the near future, I purposed to just enjoy being Mommy to my six precious children. I would be grateful for each day that I had with them. I was determined to provide an environment where the children would learn to love and serve one another, to see God's hand and provision in our lives, but also just to enjoy the little things.

Chapter 14

When Anna was not quite six years old, she called upon Jesus to be her Savior. She always talked fondly of Jesus and openly displayed her love for him, but one day, she came under conviction about her sin. It was an incredible thing to witness. Kyle was out of town on business, and the kids and I were in the kitchen talking about heaven and hell. I had placed myself on the countertop. Most of my children were either leaning against the counters or sitting on the floor. Anna, however, was on the step ladder sitting in front of me. I'm not quite sure what started the conversation, but I remember specifically telling Silas, "Those that reject Christ can't enter into heaven. They must go to a place called hell, and it's not a good place!" It was about that time that Anna began to cry uncontrollably. I thought she got hurt. I said, "Anna, what's wrong?" She just kept crying. I begged her to tell me what was wrong. Finally, she tried, "Well, it's just—," then more tears.

After several attempts she said, "I don't think God

can forgive me." I said, "Forgive you for what?" I couldn't imagine her doing anything that terrible. She then said, "I told God I hated him." I was surprised by her words. It didn't sound like something Anna would say. Puzzled, I said, "Why did you tell him that, Anna?" She then said, "When I got in trouble and you told me to go to the pantry (our discipline room), I got mad at God and told him that I hated him." Tears continued to pour out of her eyes and roll down her pudgy little cheeks. My heart felt so sad for her. What torment for a child of only five. She continued, "I don't think God can ever forgive me!" I began to wonder if Christ was drawing Anna to himself. I decided I'd better get alone with Anna and have a serious talk with her, so I took Anna to my bedroom where we could be alone.

I silently prayed that God would give me words to share that would help her to see that God truly wanted to forgive her and indeed would. I quoted Romans 3:23: "For all have sinned and come short of the glory of God." I explained to her that what she did was sin and that every person that ever lived was a sinner. She was not alone. I then told her that God certainly could forgive her and in fact wanted to. She said, "Mommy, I want to get saved, but I don't think that I can. I told God I hated him, and I don't think he can forgive that." I told her that he would remove her sin, as far as the east is from the west as it says in Psalm 103:12. She believed those words. She already knew that Jesus had died on the cross for her sins. She knew that Jesus was the Son of God, and that he came to offer himself as the final sacrifice for the sins of the world. She'd memorized scriptures and was familiar with the gospel of Jesus, so I simply reminded her of what she already knew but possibly didn't understand completely before. It wasn't until this moment in her life that she looked at herself as a sinner that needed forgiveness. She listened to me attentively, and then she told me that she wanted to pray and ask Jesus to forgive her for her sins and save her.

She came to me several times that evening seeking reassurance that God really had forgiven her. I said to her, "Anna, if Mommy did something to hurt you and then later asked your forgiveness, how would you feel if I kept saying, 'Oh, I know you can't forgive me. I'm not worthy of your forgiveness!' It would break your heart, wouldn't it? That's how God feels when you are asking forgiveness and then you are not accepting the forgiveness he has already given. He has been waiting for you to ask him to forgive you. He wants to redeem you and offer you eternal life." This little illustration worked. By bedtime, she had accepted that God had forgiven her and had delivered her from her sin. Without my prompting, she also told me that she wanted to be baptized, so I told her I'd talk to Daddy and we'd figure it out.

On July 3rd, 2004, Kyle baptized Anna in a friend's pool. She had never gone under water before, but she wasn't scared, or if she was, she didn't let on. She did tell me before we went over there that she was a little nervous, but I think it was just because she was going to be in the spotlight, with all eyes on her! It was a joyful day for all of us, and it's all captured on video. (But it's too bad the man next door was mowing his lawn!)

A couple of months after Anna turned six years old, on a Sunday evening, she had a strange episode where she couldn't catch her breath and her heart was beating very fast. I panicked, wondering what could be happening. It wasn't long before the symptoms went away, but the next morning, I noticed that she was retaining fluid in her face, arms, hands, and ankles. It was a new symptom, not something I had seen in her before. I gave her raw cabbage juice as a natural diuretic and hoped it would just go away, but I planned to call the doctor on Monday morning. The juice did work in taking the fluid off, and when we took her to Doctor Allen, her pediatric cardiologist, he checked everything out and said that she probably had too much sodium or caffeine (as I had suggested), because everything looked pretty much the same. He put her on Lasix, a diuretic, and said to watch her and to let him know if there were any changes.

Over the next few weeks, she did do better in some ways, but she just wasn't quite herself. I didn't rush her back to the doctor, because she was doing better than she had been while we were at the doctor's office, and he hadn't seen anything to be alarmed by, but I was uneasy about her health. She was tiring more easily. She was also losing her appetite a bit. I assumed that she was just recovering from whatever it was that started the symptoms. I was continually in prayer about it, but I kept this concern to myself. I didn't want to upset Anna or the rest of the family. Every time I asked her how she was feeling, she would say, "Fine." She was always careful not to make me worry. I know that part of the reason she always said she was okay is because she didn't want me to fret about her. She was amazingly aware of things that most young children would never think about.

I found myself researching on the internet ways to help her, natural ways to help thin her blood and strengthen her heart. I had her doing light exercises in hopes of strengthening her. She was happy to do them. I think it gave her hope that she might start feeling better. I was juicing fruits and vegetables for her, and she would drink carrot, spinach, and celery juice without a complaint. I still worried though, because besides her physical changes, she was also just *different*. She no longer wanted to go play outside, which was something she usually loved to do. She wanted to be by me all the time. She wanted to sit by me and sleep with me. She just seemed more serious about life, more thoughtful and pensive.

One night Anna was in bed with Kyle and me when she gently rubbed my arm with her little hands and said with a little smile, "Mommy, I'm so glad you make us laugh. You're a fun Mommy. I love you." Tears threatened to fall. Something in her touch and in her words was very strange and brought emotions that I almost couldn't control. I was so grateful for her precious words of love, but I feared them, because I wondered at God's purpose in allowing her to speak them.

Kyle had decided that he wanted to take our family to Disney World. We really couldn't afford it, but we had learned a lot about life and because of those lessons, he decided that the smiles and fun our children would have would be worth every penny! They didn't need that to be happy, but he wanted to give that gift to them. We mentioned that to our doctor at Anna's appointment. He recommended that we contact the Make-A-Wish foundation. When he made that recommendation, I looked at him with quizzical eyes. Did that mean she was dying? He read my expression and reassured me that she didn't have to be terminally ill to receive it, but it was for children with life-threatening illnesses. He said that Anna would definitely qualify to receive a wish, and if she wanted to go to Disney World, then the trip would be free! The Make-A-Wish Foundation did give Anna that trip to Disney World. Anna wanted Grandma and Grandpa to come with us, but The Make-A-Wish Foundation had a policy to only send immediate family, so my parents paid their own way and came with us. This made the trip even more fun for everybody, and it was helpful to have four extra hands to keep track of little ones in an unbelievably crowded place!

Anna needed oxygen on the airplane. It stressed me out, but she handled it very well. We enjoyed the airplane ride. Because there were so many of us, we had to spread out. I sat by Anna and kept Jonas on my lap. Traveling by plane with a party of ten is quite interesting! We were very happy to arrive at the airport in Florida. We were dressed in sweatshirts, having just left autumn weather in

Kansas, and we immediately realized how silly we were to be in such warm clothing. It was *hot!*

We stayed at a resort called Give Kids the World, and Grandma and Grandpa stayed at a nearby hotel. Give Kids the World was amazing! It is a charity that works with the Make-A-Wish foundation and other organizations like them. When we arrived, they took us into the front office and gave all the kids presents. Anna got the biggest present, and while it was very nice that their goal was to give her the time of her life, it made Anna feel a bit strange. I could read it on her face. She wasn't used to being treated better than her brothers and sisters. I think she wondered why she was getting such special treatment.

They gave the kids gifts every day. We ate for free. We had all the ice cream we wanted. It was a bright, cheery place, but it was my least favorite place to be while we were in Orlando. It's hard to explain why I felt this way, but it was like this: my little girl, whom I had always treated like the rest of my children other than her medical care, was being treated like somebody that was dying. I didn't like it. I wasn't prepared to go there in my thoughts. Nobody told me she was dying. We were just here because she qualified, not because she was terminally ill, but somehow I felt like they knew something we didn't know.

I hated facing the reality that Anna did have a very serious problem. If she hadn't had that scary episode with her heart a couple months back, and if she was still doing well, I probably wouldn't have felt this way. However, Anna was having problems. There were new things going on with her that were perplexing. She was not herself. I hated it. I didn't want my little girl to get sick and die. I wanted her by my side as long as I was on this earth. I carried this burden and worry in my heart…for me, for Kyle, for the children, and especially for her. I didn't want her to hurt. I didn't want her to be sad. I could sense that she was trying to cover up her physical problems, because she didn't want to worry me. That was just Anna. She didn't act like a six-year-old. But I consoled myself, thinking that if she was really feeling very ill, surely she would tell me. She'd always been strong, but she'd also always told me if she was sick.

Some of the best times were at Disney World. Anna was so distracted by all of the fun that her mind wasn't on her health. She smiled and laughed a lot! She didn't have a lot of energy, so she rode in the stroller most of the time, but she went on a lot of the kids' rides and especially loved the Winnie-the-Pooh ride.

She made sure she took turns riding with all of us. She took turns sitting next to each of us in the car. I noticed this, and it too made me anxious. It was as if she was preparing to leave and was attempting to put everything in order with her relationships, even her relationship with the Lord. She was spending special moments with each one of us.

She had a special request to ride the Winnie-the-Pooh ride with Cecily. She didn't want any adult in the seat with them; she just wanted Cecily and herself in the seat. The first time it didn't work out that way, and she was so disappointed. So we went on the ride again so she could have Cecily alone with her. I took a picture of her when she was on the ride. She loved it. It was a little thing, but it meant a lot to her!

The first day at Disney World she was having so much fun that she stayed awake all day! As tuckered out as she'd been, she had been napping every day, so this encouraged me. I was excited that she had the energy to stay awake until ten o'clock p.m.! I found myself looking for any little thing to make me feel that she was getting back to normal. My emotions really were out of control. My mind kept jumping back and forth. *She is dying, and she is saying goodbye* to *That's a good sign! She's going to get better!* This worry and fear was all-consuming.

Chapter 15

We returned home from Orlando after a week of fun and were attempting to settle back into some sort of routine. It was a difficult task after a week of being spoiled in every way! Nobody wanted to jump back into school and chores. Anna's health continued to decline. It began to take work to keep fluid off of her. She would wake up swollen every morning. The diuretic worked, but she couldn't keep fluid off without it. It was my goal to get her back to normal, but she had many different things going on. She would wake up in the night crying or screaming. She also had constant burping and was continuing to lose her appetite. It all seemed to happen so fast. I felt I was losing control of the situation very quickly. I mentioned to her one day, "Anna, why don't we go back to the doctor and just let him give you a quick check up." She cried, "No, Mommy. Please don't make me go." But I knew that I would need to call the doctor just as soon as Daddy got back into town.

When Kyle was traveling for a couple of days, the kids

begged me to put up the Christmas tree. We always put it up earlier than most people, but this was even earlier than usual. I called Kyle to see if he cared. He didn't, so I conceded, after much begging, and we put up the Christmas tree. It was our traditional set up. Jared (and usually Daddy) sat and watched a movie. It was usually *It's a Wonderful Life, Home Alone,* or *Ernest Saves Christmas.* I'm not sure what it was he watched that night. The rest of us were focused on the tree. We were the laborers! Jared (and usually Kyle) had the job of telling us we were doing a great job. We were having a great time! Each of the children took ornaments and placed them on the tree right next to the last one they hung, and when they weren't looking, I moved them to a better spot. The girls hung their homemade ornaments. None of us will ever forget Anna's eyes when she stood back and looked at the tree. She said, "Oh! It's just beautiful!" She, like some of the rest of us, had a flare for the dramatic.

Kyle came home the next night. The children ran to him and told him he just had to come and look at the tree! He stood and admired their work. Mindy, an adult friend that lived in our cottage on our property came over to play with the girls. It had been a while since she had been over to see us. She loved the children and liked to spend time with them. She played Old Maid with me and the little girls. She also did the Hokey Pokey and played Simon Says with us. When it was Anna's turn to lead in Simon Says, she did so good that she got somebody out, and then cried because she thought she did something wrong. We tried to encourage her by explaining that she was supposed to get us out.

We sang some songs together, and then Kyle read out of the Bible to us. It really was a perfect evening, one of those evenings that we all live for but don't often enough take time to live. After Daddy's final prayer, we did the usual kisses goodnight and all headed to our own beds.

Journal Entry
November 18th, 2004

Life is very sweet. I've had my moments where I despair and worry, but God always reminds me to count it all joy. Live today, today. After all, God's grace is sufficient and he may take us to our eternal home at any moment!

November 19th a few hours before the sunrise.

I awoke suddenly to hear my six-year-old daughter Anna loudly crying out. I glanced at the clock. It was 3:23 a.m. I threw the covers off of myself, quickly got out of bed, and hurried to her room. I was surprised to see Cecily still asleep next to her and little brother Silas still sleeping in his toddler bed next to theirs.

"What's wrong, Anna?" I asked with a frantic heart. Anxiously she said, "I don't feel well, and I *do not* know why." I wondered if she had a migraine. They were not uncommon for Anna. I'd always wondered if her lower oxygen level was a reason that she got them. "Do you have a headache?" I asked.

"No, it's not a headache. I don't know what it is, but I feel really sick." I picked her up and hurried her to the bathroom. She immediately threw up. It wasn't like other times when she'd thrown up; it was very violent and loud. It surprised me and scared me. Her heart began to beat so fast and hard, I could see her chest moving with each beat.

"Are you okay, sweetie?" I asked while gently rubbing my hands against her arms and giving her a sympathetic look. "Yes, I feel a little better. Mommy, may I please take a bath?" While Anna was in the bath, we prayed. We prayed that she would feel better and that God would take away her pain. I then sat and talked to her. It was November and Christmas was right around the corner. To get her mind off of being sick, I began to talk about Christmas presents.

"What would you like for Christmas," was my question to distract her. "A little brown box to put my treasures in, like Lydia's," she said. Lydia was one of Anna's special friends that she had just spent some time with that week. She also told me that she would like a newborn baby doll and a pretty dress. I'm not sure the distraction was working that well, but she was playing along. She wanted me to think she was feeling better, but the look in her eyes and her pale face spoke volumes.

I got her out of the tub, and she threw up again. For the moment she was feeling a little better, so I got her dressed, took her to her room, and crawled into bed with her. Her heart was beating fast which caused her breathing to be labored. I could tell that she wasn't comfortable. I began to panic a little. She had had a couple of similar episodes in the past but both of those times it lasted for a short time and then she was fine. I tried to talk myself out of worrying.

I propped myself up on some pillows and laid Anna in front of me; her back was to my tummy. She could breathe better when she wasn't flat on her back. I could feel her heart beating against me. I stroked her wavy brown hair and rubbed her soft little cheeks and her forehead. I was anxious, but I tried to breathe very slow and steady. With Anna lying against me, I thought that my own breathing pattern might affect hers.

I silently talked to God about Anna and asked him to calm my fears and make her better. I reminded him how special she was to me and how hard it was to watch her suffer. I hoped that she would relax in my arms and that her heart would slow down. It did a little.

After a few minutes she said, "I feel *so* much better now." Ah, what a relief to hear those words! I can deal with my own pain and suffering, but to have to watch my children suffer is a great burden to bear. I can't think of much that is more difficult for me.

I assumed she had the stomach flu and that the vomiting was what made her heart race, but I decided at that moment that I would call her cardiologist first thing in the morning. Somewhere deep down I wondered if there was more to it, but I wasn't prepared to go there with my thoughts. If it was her heart, the next step would probably be a heart and lung transplant. I was frightened by those thoughts.

We had enjoyed over six years with Anna, and most of those years were fairly uneventful as far as her heart was concerned. Recently things had changed in her health, but even her doctor didn't see a big change in her heart function when he had given her a thorough examination. Maybe only I noticed, but she just hadn't been herself.

After spending about fifteen minutes with Anna lying against me, Jonas, our one-year-old, woke up to nurse. He was in my bedroom, so I told Anna I would be right back. I propped her up against a few pillows and went into my bedroom. Kyle was just waking up to get ready for work, so I asked, "Honey, can you please get Anna and bring her in here? She isn't feeling well."

He went and picked her up and said, "You're not feeling well, huh?" She just shook her head and cuddled up against her Daddy's chest. He laid her in his spot on our bed, pulled the covers up over her, gave her a kiss, and went to the bathroom across the hall to get ready for work.

I had nursed Jonas for about ten minutes when Anna sat up very suddenly and screamed. It sounded like fear more than anything, but I could immediately tell she was sick. I quickly put Jonas on the bed. Thank goodness I had given him enough to satisfy him. He was awake but didn't fuss when I put him down.

I grabbed a cup that was on the nightstand and put it in front of Anna's mouth. She threw up. She continued to cry out with severe intensity. I immediately panicked.

I frantically said, "Anna, you're going to hurt yourself!" I was not only afraid of what was causing her pain and fear, but I was certain that her weak heart couldn't handle this degree of intensity for long. She then threw her head back and fell onto the bed. I tried to set her up. I was afraid she would throw up and choke on it. She wouldn't get up. In fact, I couldn't even force her up—her body was arched back and stiff.

I began to scream for Kyle…nothing…I screamed again…he still couldn't hear me! I hurried off of the bed, flipped on the light, and screamed for Kyle from the doorway. He finally heard me and came running in with fear in his eyes.

"Call 911! Hurry! Something is wrong with Anna!" I said with extreme panic in my voice.

Somehow, he remembered that the phone was in Jared's room. Of course Jared, Anna's 14-year-old brother, woke up. He ran in and saw his little sister. She looked very abnormal and was making strange noises. Kyle told him to take Jonas and go to his bedroom to pray. He quickly obeyed.

When we realized that her heart wasn't beating, Kyle and I began to do CPR. The phone call had been made. Kyle was on the phone yelling "Hurry up…oh, Anna, honey, please hang on." "You can't die, Anna. Hang on for us!" Crying, he pleaded, "Please hurry! Are you almost here? She's not breathing!" Kyle was frantic. It was all so sudden. He didn't go to bed worried like I did, and he hadn't been up with her.

We had never done CPR on a real person before,

but we had taken classes when Anna was a baby. They wouldn't let us leave the hospital with her until we had learned how to perform the procedure. I had hoped we'd never have to use those skills.

I was very quiet. I wouldn't say I was calm, because I didn't feel that way. What would be the outcome of this nightmare? From the moment it all began, I had wondered if it was Anna's time to enter heaven. I guess it could have been God giving me a resolve in my spirit, but I didn't trust my feelings and, in fact, rejected them. I was nervous and somewhat frantic in my thoughts, yet there was a strange peace as well.

It's kind of hard to describe all that was going through my mind. Kyle was doing chest compressions, and I was attempting to breathe life into my little girl. I did it without saying a word, but my whole body trembled. It was difficult to perform this necessary task, because I was breathing like any person who was in shock and panicked. My breaths were quick and shallow.

Kyle cried and begged the man on the phone to get somebody to our house and pleaded with God and with Anna. He was desperate. I felt every emotion he was feeling, but I let him verbalize it. I remained quiet.

After doing CPR for what seemed like an eternity, Anna's heart began to beat very slowly. Her eyes that had been looking towards us began to look the other direction as though she was looking at something else. Perhaps there was something more precious to see on her other side. I began to sing to her. "Jesus loves me this I know. For the Bible tells me so. Little ones to him belong. They are weak but he is strong." I said, "Anna, Jesus is right here with you. Don't be afraid. He will take care of you, honey. I love you, I love you, I love you." Her heart quit beating.

Our sweet little daughter was gone. We would not hear her voice or see her sweet little smiling face or cuddle her soft warm body again until we were together again in heaven.

That beautiful evening on November 18th, 2004, was our last one with our precious Anna Gabrielle. She was gone from us, not forever, but for now. I stood in awe when I read my journal entry from that night. I was amazed that the very night before Anna died, God had given me an eternal perspective. He knew I would need it. It makes me feel very close to my Lord. I know that he loved me enough to purposely put that thought into my head so I would be able to look back and see his hand in it all.

After we had given up all hope and accepted that Anna was not coming back to us, we stayed at the hospital for a while. We had friends show up to minister to our broken hearts. It was seven o'clock a.m. It was time to go home and share the tragic news with our children, Anna's brothers and sisters.

When we walked into our door, my Mom and Dad were there with Jared and Jonas. They met us at the door with tears and hugs. We clung together. We were all filled with sorrow and couldn't say anything to each other. I hurt for me and for Kyle and for my parents, but I hurt mostly for our children. Why did they have to hurt like this? No child should have to experience this type of loss. It just seemed so unfair.

We all sat down and Kyle went upstairs to wake up Abigail and Cecily. When they walked down the stairs, they looked at us funny. They saw my parents and must have wondered why they were there so early in the morning. I saw Abigail's eyes begin to search the room. I wondered if she was looking for Anna. Kyle didn't want to beat around the bush. It was going to be a big blow no matter how he said it, and they would begin to notice that Anna wasn't here and begin to ask questions any moment. So Kyle quickly said, "Last night Anna got sick. This morning she got very sick and she went to be with Jesus." Their reactions broke my heart. Abigail had a lost look as she began to weep. Cecily said, "No!" and began to run up the stairs. We grabbed her and held her close and let her cry until there were no more tears (at least for a while). Later we asked her why she ran up the stairs, and she said "Because, I wanted to prove to you guys that Anna was still upstairs in bed."

Jared sat very quietly. I could only imagine what was going through his mind. No child should have to watch three siblings die. I know that these losses have affected Jared deeply, but I also know that God has used these heartaches to make him strong and tender. The burdens he has had to bear have made him a more thoughtful person. Sometimes he fears things more than others because that "worst case scenario" that doesn't happen to most people, has happened to him (us) three times. It is easy to be a worrier when you've experienced those types of things in life. This has been a bit of a challenge for all of us. He later told me that while we were at the hospital he was on his knees crying his heart out and begging the Lord to spare Anna's life.

I'm not sure Silas and Jonas fully grasped what was going on. In fact, I know they didn't. Their smiles and silliness were one way that God kept us smiling through a time when we normally wouldn't have been able to.

Jared went back to the hospital with us. I wasn't sure it was a good idea, but he wanted to, and I didn't want to regret anything. It was a really bad time to be faced with a lot of decisions, but there were a lot of decisions to make.

We had been asked if we wanted to donate any of Anna's organs. Because of her heart problems, the only thing they would allow to be donated was her eyes, specifically her corneas. We knew that she would have wanted this. Anna would have gladly given anything to help others.

When we went home to tell our children about Anna, our friends stayed at the hospital with her. My friend Renee said, "I just couldn't leave her there alone." So, when we went back, some of our friends were still there. We talked and remembered Anna's sweet ways as we stared at her lifeless, but still precious body. We all touched her. Jared held her hand and touched her face. When we got ready to leave, he reached for her hair and messed it up and said, "Bye, Pookie." This was something he did often. It was so precious and yet so hard to watch. I hugged him and cried with him. We left to go back home and face this horrible trial together.

As the day drug on, our house was filled with family members and friends that wanted to support us in our heartache. I wish I could have shown appreciation for their visits. I walked around in a daze and felt so inadequate to show my love for them. People brought food, gave big hugs and asked what they could do to help. I was numb and probably appeared so to all of them. I wonder what it looked like from where they were. Bless their hearts. It took courage to come to us at that time. I've chickened out many times in similar situations and don't ever plan to again.

That first day, we were so busy dealing with the business of Anna's death, that we couldn't take much time to mourn. I don't think we ever stopped crying, but we had to take care of the arrangements for the memorial service, and we were still in shock. Our deep mourning would have to wait until we could be alone. My sister Lisa and her husband Brad drove us to the funeral home. I was grateful Kyle and I didn't have to go alone. After going through the difficult process of choosing a casket and talking about details of the funeral, there was a question that really slapped the reality of this whole situation in my face. For the obituary, the man asked me the names of our remaining children. I began, "Jared, Abigail,

Cecily—" It was at this point I would have routinely said, "Anna." I now had to skip over her name for the first time. A feeling of fear came over me. Would I be able to do it? Could I just skip over her? I looked across the table at my sister. There was a sincere look of compassion. I put my head down on the table and wept.

The next day, the first morning without Anna was unbelievably sad. I woke up very early and immediately felt the emptiness and deep pain. There was a real physical pain involved as well as an emotional pain. I needed Kyle. I knocked on the bathroom door where he was. It was about four o'clock a.m. He opened the door, and we both just began to cry. We sat on the bathroom floor together and wept bitterly and said hopeless things to one another. At that moment we both just wanted to die. We didn't even attempt to lift each other up. We just stayed down there together. It was our first moment of mourning together. It was only the Lord's strength that gave us enough courage to get up off that floor.

The children all had friends over, which really helped them through the following days. Their friends kept them somewhat preoccupied for a few days, and it didn't really sink in. This was good because it gave Kyle and me time to gain the strength to help them. We thanked God for this distraction for them.

Abigail didn't want her friends at first, she just wanted me. I'll never forget when she came upstairs and laid down next to me, and we just cuddled up together and cried. I was happy to be there for her, but neither one of us could offer each other anything more than physical affection. We hugged and held hands and cuddled. But, in time, her friends did a good job of coaxing her to have some fun. They took Abigail and Cecily shopping and out to eat. In the midst of sadness they actually had some fun, and I'm so glad they did, because I knew we had a long road ahead.

God gave our children a great peace during the first couple of days. Jared's friend Timothy was a good distraction for him. Jared would come over and check on me and Kyle. He'd ask how we were doing and give us a hug, and then when he was satisfied that we were okay for the moment, he'd go back to his friend. It was obvious it was the Lord's strength that he was experiencing. Cecily hugged everybody. She lost her best friend, yet she was offering comfort to others. She kept saying, "You still have me, Mom." It was a true miracle that Cecily was doing okay. Anna was her companion in everything. They shared a bedroom, played together, did school together, etc. They truly were inseparable. She had to be missing her so much, yet she was holding up and ministering to us! God was ministering to our sweet children in a very special way. He was giving them peace that only he could give.

Chapter 16

Anna was just learning to read and write, so she had begun writing notes to us. I remembered a note that Anna had written to me, but I couldn't remember where I put it. I was driven into a frenzy looking for it. What if I could never find that sweet note that she had given to me just a few days before? I had people looking all over the house for it. When at last I found it, I rejoiced and thanked God for giving that note to me. It said:

Mommy, I love you.
You are pritee.
Love, Anna

She had not only written one to me but also to her daddy and Cecily. Now we all had our own special notes. We will cherish them forever!

We worked non-stop from Saturday until Monday

morning to prepare for Anna's memorial service. Part of us wanted to crawl in a hole and let somebody else plan the service, but a larger part of us wanted this to be a celebration of Anna's life, and everything had to be perfect! On Monday there would be a memorial service that would allow people that didn't know Anna well the opportunity to wish they had known her and would give those that knew her and loved her the satisfaction of knowing that there were a lot of good reasons to miss her and look forward to seeing her again.

Kyle felt that God wanted him to speak at the memorial service and mentioned it to my dad and a friend of ours. They were glad to hear that, and they both encouraged it. As he meditated on what he would say, he began to chicken out. He didn't think he'd have the strength to get through it. He felt sure that it would be all right to back out, but when he mentioned that to these same two people, they begged him to reconsider. Since they didn't let him off the hook, he began to put some words together to share and asked God to let him know whether it was required of him. He knew in his heart that it was.

I was putting together a DVD of family videos and pictures of Anna's life. I worked on it practically non-stop. I didn't sleep for two days. I was on a mission, and even though that included viewing videos and pictures of Anna, God helped me not to fall apart. God gave me supernatural strength. I was so busy with the technicalities of it all that I didn't take time to be sad. I just worked.

Satan was at work too. Everything that could go wrong

went wrong at the last minute. The memorial service was at 10 o'clock a.m. Here it was Monday morning and the material that I had all put together would not burn on a DVD. We tried everything, and we were running out of time! Kyle stopped and said, "Okay, Satan, you are officially resisted!" He went back to the computer and the DVD began to burn! Hallelujah! He had also asked my Aunt Judy, who had just called, to pray for us and she did with him, right there on the phone.

We got that done and Kyle printed his notes for his speech. We made sure we had all the children and literally ran out the door. We were running very late for our own daughter's funeral.

On the way to the church, which was forty minutes away, Kyle realized that the printer didn't print the last two pages of his notes! If he had any confidence at all, it began to leave him at that moment. There was no time to go back. I pulled out some paper and began to question him about what he had typed up. I had read his notes so I thought between the two of us we could remember, and then I would write it down for him. Neither one of us could remember a thing, so he asked me to pray that God would give him the words to say. And I'm here to tell you that the words that God gave him were wonderful, probably even better than what he'd written down. God obviously had it all planned. It was the Holy Spirit that spoke through Kyle that day.

There were several hundred people at the service. I didn't really pay much attention to who was there. I didn't want to draw any attention to myself. I was there to share Anna with others. I wanted her to be the star of the show! We began with singing some songs that Anna liked. We sang, "Isn't it Wonderful to be a Christian" and "He's Able." My only complaint is that the songs were played way too slow, not technically, but compared to how we sang them. As a family we sang these songs very cheerfully and fun, and often with silly accents. I almost said out loud in front of hundreds of people, "Speed it up!" I held back, but I wish now that we would have sung them correctly, well, Kraft family style. Some friends of ours sang Anna's favorite song, "A Passion for Thee," and the children of the church sang, "Jesus Loves Me." This song has been sung at all three of our children's memorial services, and each time by the children in the church. There really is something special about children singing at a child's funeral. I felt like they were singing to Anna.

It was time for Kyle to get up and speak. He went up to the podium without tears and without hesitation. I envisioned Jesus leading Kyle to the podium and then standing with his hand on Kyle's shoulder the whole time he was speaking. Kyle spent about fifteen to twenty minutes sharing his heart, sharing Anna's life. He spoke of her character, her strength, her silliness, her weaknesses, her joy, her love for Jesus, and everything else he could think of concerning Anna. He spoke of our love for her. He shared about the precious notes that she had written just a few days before. He shared lessons about perspective and memories. It was just perfect! It was a beautiful reflection of Anna's life through her daddy's eyes and heart.

When Kyle was done, he came to sit by me. Immediately he slumped his shoulders and wept silently at my side. The strength was there when he needed it, just as God proclaims in his word it will be! I was so very proud of my strong husband. That had to be one of the most difficult things a father could ever have to do, but with God by his side, he did it! The memorial service was just as we hoped it would be; a beautiful reflection of our precious daughter Anna.

Part 2: My Walk with Grief

When you read books or articles on grieving, you generally read about the steps or stages of grief. It is likely that grieving individuals share many of the same emotions feelings and even stages, but each person and situation is unique. Not everybody gets angry. Not every person asks why. Some losses create deep, painful sorrow, while others might create more of a bittersweet sorrow. Perhaps like the death of a 95-year-old grandparent who has already watched their spouse die and was looking forward to going home to heaven.

Everybody is unique. Different personalities cope with death in different ways. Individual circumstances create a variety of emotions and feelings. Rest assured, all sorrow hurts. Every person will suffer the affliction of loss at some point, except perhaps a child that dies at a young age, but no person, book, or article can provide complete comfort and understanding, because nobody will ever know exactly how *you* feel...except for Jesus. He not only knows you are hurting but knows the deep emotions of *your* heart. His compassions, they fail not! Jesus knows your pain and desires your prayers so that he can answer them.

This part of the book is my story of what I experienced, as I mourned the loss of Anna. It was different from when I mourned the loss of my babies. I grieved all three times, but experiencing the loss of my six-year-old was more severe for me. I was not only missing what could have been but what had been. I was not only wishing I had been able to hold her, but my body craved her embrace and her touch. I wanted to hug her, move her hair away from her eyes, help her with her zipper, and kiss her goodnight; things I had done so many times before. This is my personal walk with grief.

Fresh Sorrow

Anna's sudden death threw us into our trial very quickly. One night we went to bed and all was well, and seven hours later we were saying our final goodbyes to our precious Anna. Our road took a sharp turn, and we were now headed down this path called sorrow. It held many challenges for our family.

Have you ever walked into a room and couldn't remember what you went in there for? As you stand there wracking your brain, you begin to feel as if you're losing your mind. It leaves you with a feeling of confusion. That's a good way to describe how I felt at almost every moment during the days following Anna's death. Life was very surreal. I kept thinking I was going to wake up from a bad dream and that Anna would just be here and life would be back to normal. I was in a constant daze. Many times we'd be going somewhere or doing something together, and I would suddenly feel like I forgot Anna. A surge of panic would rush through me.

Some of the thoughts that entered my mind didn't

make any sense. I was filled with guilt, because I felt like I had abandoned Anna and sent her off to be alone. I had visions of her in heaven wandering around with nobody else in sight, and I would begin to cry and tell my friends and family that Anna needed me. I had taken care of her for over six years, but now I couldn't do anything for her. I wasn't asked, I was forced to accept that she was in God's full-time care now, and he didn't need me to care for her any longer.

I consider each of my children precious gifts from the Creator and I marvel that he used me to create them and to care for them. He even gave them some of my features so they would look like me (although most of them look more like Kyle). I know that my children don't really belong to me, but when Anna died, I felt like something that I owned had been taken away.

When Hannah gave her son Samuel back to God by giving him to Eli the priest, she was making a conscious decision. She had committed to do that before he was even born. While I'm sure it was a difficult day when she left her son, she was confident in her choice. Even though I had committed Anna to God's care, I felt that this was against my will. This was not my choice, and I didn't feel good about Anna being gone. I knew that God was the one that sustained her life as long as he did, and I give him full credit for that and praise him for being her strength, but that doesn't mean I was prepared to say goodbye so suddenly. If God would have asked me for permission before he took her, I truly hope that I would have been willing, but I was not at that point of acceptance just yet. I needed time to fully grasp the idea of Anna being gone before I could accept it.

My spirit knew that the things floating through my mind were far from truth. I know that heaven isn't empty. I also know that Anna doesn't need me. She may desire my presence in heaven, but not in the same way that I desire hers here on earth. I had to listen to others as they spoke truth to me. Usually all it took was a reminder of the truth, many times over, and I believed it. When you are grieving, your mind doesn't necessarily think accurately. I certainly wasn't in my right mind while I was grieving.

I blamed myself for not taking better care of Anna. I did everything I knew to do. I gave her all of her heart medicines faithfully. I juiced vegetables for her and fed her a healthy diet. I made sure she got plenty of fresh air and sunshine. I helped her to do moderate exercise, but I always kept her from playing too hard. Despite all this, I still had feelings of guilt. I asked myself questions like, *Would she still be alive if I would have thought to have her chew up an aspirin or two that morning she was sick, to thin her blood? Would she have continued to do well if I would have had her on an even stricter diet? Was there some natural thing that I could have given her to help strengthen her heart? If I would have taken her to the hospital or called 911 right away when I realized she was sick, would they have been able to do something to help her?*

They were sad thoughts that confused me and gave me a very unsettled feeling. Deep down, I knew that it was God's appointed time for Anna to leave this earth. No matter what I did, it wouldn't have changed things.

There was an element of peace in knowing that even in the midst of my confusion. It was her appointed time, but in my grief, I didn't always remember the truth. It took time to accept what had happened and especially to realize that it was final. Anna would not be coming home.

Life Goes On As Usual For the Rest of the World

Kyle took me to the mall to get a dress for the memorial service. This was no desire of my own, but he thought it might be a good idea to get out of the house. I would usually enjoy shopping for a new dress, but it brought me no joy that day. I was so lost in my sadness that I really didn't care what I was wearing. It was the last thing on my mind. Every outfit I tried on looked terrible to me. More distressing however was observing the people around me that were unaffected by my affliction.

I viewed my surroundings through tear-filled eyes. I noticed people laughing and just kind of hangin' out. People were ordering pretzels and sodas, hollering at their children, and really doing regular, everyday stuff. On an uneventful day, when everything was going well, I wouldn't even have noticed. That day I did.

People shouldn't be laughing. My little girl just died. People shouldn't be arguing. My little girl just died. People shouldn't even be enjoying food! I wanted to scream out, "Stop! My daughter, whom I loved with all of my heart, just died!" How could life just continue without a thought of me and my sorrow?

It was just so strange that I was feeling more sadness than I'd ever felt, and yet, life didn't stop to notice. People didn't know what had just happened to me. They couldn't read my pain. They couldn't feel my hurt. My life and sorrow were nothing to them.

I wonder how many times I've walked by someone that just found out they had cancer or just lost a loved one. Is it possible that I confused their dazed look for rudeness? Was their blank stare one of heartache? Is it possible that my little smile could encourage them in their sorrow? Perhaps that smile would be one that would make them open up and share what was on their heart, and I could touch their life with a word of encouragement.

On occasion, a smile or a greeting enticed me to open up to a cashier or a shopper. If they said, "How are you today," and they seemed like someone that was truly interested, sometimes I'd tell them that I was heartbroken because my daughter had just died. Many times the only thing they could say was, "I'm sorry," and that was the end of the conversation. Other times they'd ask questions, and I would be given an opportunity to show pictures of Anna and talk about what a blessing she was.

When I was picking out curtains for a music room in our home that we were creating in honor of Anna, the lady helping me asked me about the room. I told her that our six-year-old daughter had just died, and she loved to sing and play piano, so we were putting together a music room in her honor. She began to cry. I could tell her heart was truly touched. I showed her pictures and talked about Anna. It turned out she had a young son with heart problems too. Her son went to the same pediatric cardiologist that Anna had gone to. I was glad that I met her. I've seen her a couple times since that day. She doesn't remember me now, but that's okay. There may be a day when I will approach her and tell her how grateful I was that day when she gave me an opportunity to share my little girl with her.

On another occasion, when we were shopping for a cedar chest for Anna's things, the old man in the store was less than cheery. He just stood there and looked at us. He didn't offer help. He didn't make any recommendations. His brief comments gave us the impression that he didn't care whether we bought the cedar chest from him or not. I wondered if he might soften a bit if I told him why we needed the cedar chest. I really did like the chest, and his price, but I knew I wouldn't be able to buy from him if he didn't brighten his countenance just a little. So, I told him we were purchasing the cedar chest to put our daughter's things in, because she had recently died. He coldly said, "If it's not what you're looking for, then don't buy it." This man does have a reputation in town for being less than friendly, but I was a bit shocked that he was so completely unaffected by my statement. Maybe he thought I was just using that as an excuse to get him to come down on the price. I suppose some people would stoop that low on occasion to save money. Needless to say, we didn't buy from him that day, even though his price was good. I feel sorry for the man and wonder what it is that makes him bitter and rude. Perhaps we should have bought the chest from him. Maybe it would have helped him in some way. I'll never know.

One of my dearest friends went to the store to get something for us the day Anna died. She said that when she was at the register checking out, the cashier asked, "How are you today?" and she said, "My friends little girl died today." She was hurting too and she hated that life didn't stop for our grief. Months later when her mother-in law died, she experienced the same thing. In fact, even sunshine annoyed her. She said it should be a rainy, gray day for the way she felt. I personally appreciated the sunshine, as the gray days made my misery greater, but for her it just didn't feel right to be enjoying sunshine in her sorrow.

It's something that I don't think you can prepare yourself for. It's just so difficult to witness life outside your own when you've just experienced a painful loss. People really do just go about their business as usual, and it's very hard to see that your huge loss really didn't matter to the majority of the world.

Emotional Release

The days following Anna's death, were mixed with a lot of things, but mostly sadness, crying, physical heartache, depression, and all the other pitiful emotions of death. It is such a sad thing to have to experience, and no matter what the situation, it just seems so unfair to have to deal with it.

I wrote in my journal a lot. It was important to have a consistent release that didn't have to involve others. Sometimes I just expressed my heart, and other times I penned my prayers or my reflections of scripture.

Looking back on those days following Anna's death, I remember my emotions being out of control and my heart feeling physically sick. My initial reaction to that memory is that I hope God never calls me to that kind of sorrow again. But as soon as I have those thoughts, I remember the closeness I shared with God and the way I clung to him as though clinging to life, and there is sweetness in that memory. I remember crying daily;

not wanting to do normal things like eat or go to the grocery store. Everyday life was a struggle. However, I'm glad that I wrote in my journal, because as I re-read my entries, I realize that, yes, I was hurting and was desperate at times, but God was showing me a part of himself and myself that I had never seen before. It was indeed hard, but it was worth the lessons that I learned. I was gaining experience, hope, and joy and tasting the sweetness of the Lord.

Journal Entry
November 29th, 2004

These past ten days have been the most difficult days of my life! The pain is so strong, and the sorrow is so intense. I miss Anna so much. So many things we do feel so different without her. I keep hearing her cute little voice and remembering things she said and did.

It's worth every bit of pain just to have her near my heart. It seems impossible that the pain will ever go away, but God has promised us in his word that it will, so I believe him. The Psalms, once again, have been a great comfort to me.

Hear, O LORD, and have mercy upon me: LORD, be thou my helper. Thou hast turned for me my mourning into dancing; thou hast put off my sackcloth, and girded me with gladness; To the end that my glory may sing praise to thee, and not be silent. O Lord my God, I will give thanks unto thee forever.

Psalm 30:10–12

This hasn't happened yet, but I praise God it will. I will hope in his mercy! Yesterday morning the Psalm that I needed was, "I shall not die, but live, and declare the works of the Lord."

I know that this painful trial will end in victory. I will do more than just barely survive. I will be able to rejoice in God's greatness. I will be able to offer comfort and hope to others someday. In the meantime, I wholly trust in my loving Lord. I will lean heavily on his strong arms, and I rest in his loving care.

Thoughts of Heaven Bring Comfort

On numerous occasions God showed me scriptures or let me meditate on thoughts of heaven, and it's truly amazing how much I was comforted on those occasions. How often do we look at the sky and begin to wonder what heaven will be like? Have you ever looked out at a field of flowers and pictured it without the weeds or bugs? Have you ever looked at your own home with chipped paint, old shingles, cracked cement, and a yard full of mud and began to envision it with fresh paint, a beautiful new wood shingle roof, a lush green yard with flowering shrubs, fruit trees (with perfect fruit), and a white picket fence to top it all off? It places us somewhere else and gives us a vision for our future home. It's a beautiful moment. I believe that it's God's desire for us to take time to dwell *in* heaven, if only for a moment here and there. He wants us to look forward to spending our eternity with him.

Thoughts of heaven can lift us from our pit and give us hope. When I found myself stooped low in sorrow,

I forced myself to looked up and envision where Anna was living. My vision wouldn't be accurate, but I could at least picture her in surroundings that made me happy. Often we feel like since we don't know what heaven will be like, we can't even take a moment to wonder. We say things like, "Oh, it doesn't matter. Whatever it is, it will be wonderful!" While I understand the truth of that type of statement, I also feel it wants for something more.

When we get ready to go to a new place, do we just get ready to go without thinking about what it might be like? If you were planning a trip to England, and you had never been there before, would you just pack your bags and make the arrangements without a thought of what it might look like or what food you might eat? I wouldn't. I would research the culture and envision the surroundings. A good part of the fun in getting ready for a vacation is dreaming of what it might be like and trying to grab hold of a visual. Why do we feel we can't do that with heaven?

I read Randy Alcorn's book called *Heaven*. I really appreciated his view, and it caused me to think about Anna's new home and my future dwelling in a totally new way. The way he imagines heaven is beyond anything I had ever considered.

Our world is a sinful place, but that doesn't mean that everything in it is bad. Everything on this earth is touched with sin, but that only means that flowers will be prettier in heaven, not absent. Our eyesight will be clearer. The grass will be greener. Joy will be greater. Love will be purer. If we take time to wonder at heaven, we can start by looking at what is in front of us and imagining it without the influence of sin.

I began to imagine what Anna might be doing. I got excited when I realized that she was there with her two brothers that she'd never met before. This gave me true joy! She talked about her brothers that she'd never met quite often and looked forward to meeting them. It was funny to realize that she now knew them better than I ever did. I was never privileged with the opportunity to spend time with them and get to know them. It's hard to picture her being there with her big brothers, because even though she was born later, I only knew them as babies, and I knew her as a little girl.

Anna loved flowers. She loved running, although with her heart problems she was limited in how far or fast she could run. Singing and playing piano were both things that she spent a lot of time doing, and they made her happy. As I began to picture this wonderful place she was in, I would close my eyes and build a whole scene in my mind. On one occasion it might have looked something like this: *Anna is standing in the midst of a huge field of beautiful flowers. The gentle wind is moving her long, dark, wavy hair, and her full-length pure white dress is also blowing in the breeze. She's singing in perfect pitch and with the purest voice. Her countenance is lovely. Her brothers are standing a little ways off watching her. They are also dressed in all white. Their hair is also dark and shines with the most beautiful radiance. The expression on their faces' is one of love and admiration for their sister. They listen as she rehearses a song she will present to Jesus.* I would leave that picture there in my mind, and it would carry me through another difficult moment.

I wonder how I would have felt during this time if I wouldn't have had the wonderful knowledge of Anna being with the Lord. Surely the God of all comfort would encourage and heal the heart of somebody grieving in this situation as well. I've known many people who have lost loved ones who didn't know Christ, and while I'm sure there is another element of acceptance and healing involved, God would be no less present. Circumstances don't limit God. He gives us everything we need to be content in our situation, no matter how impossible it seems to us. "For with God, nothing shall be impossible."

Journal Entries:
November 30th, 2004

It's another new day. I don't feel quite as sad as I did yesterday, but still there is a deep longing in my heart. I want to show Anna the snow that covers the earth this morning, but she's beholding the beauty of heaven and God's glory! She loves snow, but the cold that comes with the snow has always been hard for Anna. She will no longer be too cold or too hot. She's perfectly warmed in heaven. It's beautifully lit by the glory of God—no darkness or night—no fears or sadness—no pain.

Life is but a vapor...soon I will experience worshipping my Lord without sin. I'll worship

God while beholding his beauty in perfection—without the curse of sin.

I will talk to Anna, Samuel, and Josiah and others that are there. Together we'll declare his goodness, his majesty, his holiness. I'm sure we'll never tire of it.

Psalm 90:12 & 17: "So teach us to number our days, that we may apply our hearts to wisdom....And let the beauty of the LORD our God be upon us; and establish thou the work of our hands upon us; yea, the work of our hands establish thou it.

December 2nd, 2004

Silas asked to go to the zoo tonight, and it was a very sudden reminder that Anna wasn't here. One of the last things she asked to do was go to the zoo. I felt panic, like when you realize that you forgot something very important. I fought against the feelings while I quickly got ready for bed. I asked Jared and Abigail to pray for me, and then I got into bed and gave in to more intense grieving. I cried so hard and deep. Kyle came in and held me and once again began to remind me that Anna was in heaven, happier than I could even imagine. I shared my fears with him. I feel as though I won't ever heal. I'm scared to face the future without my precious little daughter. I want to be joyful and excited to teach the children, to go to the zoo, to go on vacations, but I can't imagine doing those things without Anna.

Kyle talked and talked to me until I was encouraged. I rejoiced in my heart as I thought of Anna alive in heaven. I can picture her playing piano, singing to the Lord, running through beautiful flowers, and talking (with her hands) to Samuel, Josiah, Grandma Tate, Grandma and Grandpa Kraft, and even Mary, Joseph, Lydia, Esther but most precious of all, I picture her talking to Jesus! She's surrounded by those that love Christ. She's never alone. She's in the midst of God's beautiful Kingdom. And God's castles are better than Cinderella's!

I woke up this morning to see the sun rise once again. It was a reminder of God's power and majesty. I know I'll break down again and again, but when I am weak, then he is strong for me. II Cor. 12:10

December 4th, 2004

I didn't cry last night! I was very peaceful. Thanks be to God! I feel at peace this morning as well. Thanks be to God! A verse that really spoke to me yesterday was Psalm 27:14, "Wait on the LORD: be of good courage, and he shall strengthen thine heart: wait, I say on the LORD."

The message I got was that God will strengthen my heart if I have courage. I can't decide to fall apart. I need to have courage. Mourning and grieving are inevitable, but courage will pull me out of it.

God's beginning to give me a better vision of Anna's dwelling. No, I can't exactly picture it, but according to scripture, I know it's beautiful, full of saints, bright, has plants and trees, has flowing water, has precious gems of different colors, gold as clear as glass, and that there are pleasures ever more!

Anna is with her Savior! Anna is worshipping and serving God in perfection!

Remembering Means Pain

There were times when grief overwhelmed us all and made for some very difficult days, but miraculously, most of the time we weren't all terribly sad at the same time. For instance, if Cecily was having a bad day, usually I was having a good one. God knew that we needed each other to get through this.

We all cried, and we all sulked and felt sorry for ourselves, but because we all have a distinct role in our family, and because we are all unique, we all dealt with our sorrow individually. Likely, I don't even know some of the things my husband and children did to cope with their pain, and I don't think they know about all of my clever escapes. None of us wanted to just let it out and cause even greater distress in the family, so we really had to be creative.

Often I would make my way to our pantry for a very quick (and quiet) outburst of emotions. If I was there too long, somebody was certain to find me, so I tried to let it out just enough to be okay for a while. Sometimes I needed to release a bigger pocket of emotions, and that's when I'd go for a country drive. On these drives, I would find a quiet dirt road with no houses in sight, and then I'd pull the car over and really let it all out! My release would often be so intense that I worried what somebody might think if they pulled up and saw (or heard) me. It was well worth the risk of being taken to the insane asylum, because the release somehow refreshed my spirit and gave me courage to go on yet another day.

There were times I'd catch Jared staring off into space and I'd ask, "Jared, are you all right?" If he wasn't, he'd say something like, "It really stinks that Anna's not here," or "How long do you think it will be before we aren't sad anymore?" I wished I could just stop and cry with him, but as his Mom, I felt it was my duty to lift him out of his pit, so I'd say, "You know what? It seems impossible that we are ever going to feel better, but we will! God will heal us more and more every day. He says he'll turn our mourning into dancing, so he will! Hang in there, sweetie. You're doing great. Momma's here. Always feel free to come and talk to me. I love you." I'd say it all with courage and confidence in my voice, and then I'd go off and pray silently for strength, because while I knew all those things I said were true, I too was wondering how and when we were going to be all right.

I wrote in my journal almost daily, Jared and Kyle wrote songs and poems. These were ways we could express what was in our heart when we didn't have the energy or ability to speak of it. This is a poem that Kyle wrote in the early days of our grief:

Oh, Anna!
Blessed pain so bittersweet,
When most I hurt, she's nearest me.
Pain, of aching, empty night,
Sweet, the mem'ry of her light.
Jesus, heal my broken heart,
Fuse that which is torn apart.
Vapor swiftly flowing by,
Soon we'll meet with You on high.

-Anna's Daddy

There were days when we would be missing Anna so much we'd just have to find something of hers to touch. It would help us to grab onto a memory. Sometimes the vivid memory would create a greater longing, but there were times that we needed it anyway. One time I remember sitting up in our attic and holding onto a little shoe, size 9 1/2. It was Anna's denim clog that she wore when she was five. She had such tiny feet! I just held it and talked to Anna. I remembered how cute she looked in those little fashionable clogs with her bell bottom pants. I talked out loud and prayed. It hurt, but it was a moment I'll never forget.

At times, I'd find both Jared and Abigail going through pictures of Anna on the computer when they were feeling sad. The children and I would kneel at the cedar chest that held Anna's special things and just go through things one by one. We'd all pick up something special and enjoy telling a story. Cecily has some of the funniest stories! She and Anna did things that I never knew about!

Abigail would listen to music that made her cry, and I wondered why she would put herself through the torture, yet I would sometimes get in the car and listen to songs that made me cry too. I would even go back and listen to a song two or three times, just so I could really get the emotion out. It felt horrible and yet it was a release. Kyle would purposely have "Pookie" memories while traveling because he needed to cry. He said he would literally sob until he was exhausted.

Kyle and I try to get a night out together once a week now that our children are old enough to babysit, but after Anna died every time we went out we'd end up in tears at some point as we'd talk about our precious daughter. It hurt so badly to talk about what we were missing, but we continued to torture ourselves week after week.

Why would we put ourselves in situations where we knew we would be sad? I think we knew that we would have to go through it all until it just didn't come anymore, so most of the time we didn't try to avoid it. It really is worth every bit of the pain it causes to see Anna at play while watching a video or having a sweet memory.

Jonas is our biggest reminder of Anna. Things he does and his expressions remind us of Anna all the time. He's like a little boy version of her. We are grateful for this because he lives with us every day.

Journal Entry:
December 5th, 2004

Last night I went shopping with Abigail and Cecily. We went to get some Christmas presents for the boys. We missed Anna and cried together. A girl's night out just isn't the same without one of the girls. But we talked about her being in heaven and talked about being with her in heaven someday, and our spirits were lifted.

Kyle is truly my knight in shining armor. His faithfulness as a husband and father and his ability to hold us together through such difficult times truly amazes me. I'm so grateful for his ability to comfort me, and I'm also grateful that he will allow his heart to seep so that I can comfort him.

Jared has been so strong through this trial. He's been more concerned about my heart than his, and he's been so helpful, playing with the boys and being so sweet to Cecily. He's a good friend to Abigail and helps her just by hangin' out with her. I'm proud of my strong young man!

Abigail is a very courageous young lady. I know she misses Anna as much as anybody, yet she continually asks me if I'm okay. She has her moments of sorrow, but she doesn't stay there long. She's always looking for something for us to do to get our minds off of our sadness. She'll often bring a game in to play. I love her with all my heart.

God is watching over Cecily. There is just no doubt about it. I worry about her because this is such a big thing for such a little girl. Her best friend in life is gone. She must often be lonely. She's been clinging to me, and I'm glad that I can be here for her. She's doing a good job being strong. I'm so proud of her.

Silas and Jonas are playing together more. They chase each other and giggle. They both like to push the dolly stroller. It's so funny to see them fight over it! Silas usually says, "Okay, you can have a turn." But then he'll go back to it a few minutes later and say, "Okay, it's my turn," and Jonas throws a fit. It's cute but pitiful (that they are playing with a dolly stroller!).

Silas walks around like he's Captain Hook. He's always humming movie music. He's so much like Jared. He says, "Yeah, sure," when you ask him for something, and he's really good about saying thank you. Grandpa told him one day how proud he was of him for being so polite and Silas said, "Thank you."

As I grieved in my journal, I also determined to write about the days events. Writing about my little boys and commenting on their play in my journal was a way to get my mind off of my pain, but it also meant that I was not ignoring these sweet little boys. I was noticing their precious play and capturing the memory in my journal. I didn't want to miss this time in their lives or in my other children's. Life doesn't stop for sorrow. I wanted to be careful that I didn't miss too much. I am so grateful for all the precious time with Anna that I can reflect on and remember.

Journal Entry Continued

Luke 1:37 and 38, "For with God nothing shall be impossible. And Mary said, Behold the handmaid of the LORD; be it unto me according to thy word."

LORD, you may do with me whatever you desire. I know that whatever you bring into my life, whoever you take from me, whatever pain you allow in my life, it's because you want me to be closer to you.

Psalm 119: 67&68–71&72:

Before I was afflicted I went astray, but now have I kept thy word. Thou art good and doest good: teach me thy statutes....It is good for me that I have been afflicted that I might learn thy statutes. The law of thy mouth is better unto me than thousands of gold and silver.

Verse 74 says, "They that fear thee will be glad when they see me, because I have hoped in thy word."

Lord, because you've allowed this painful trial in my life, I know you're not only going to get me through it, but you'll give me great victory in the end. Tonight my heart is aching for my little girl. It helps to know that she isn't just gone from me but is in your presence. I can tell that I haven't seen her, touched her, or talked to her in over two weeks. I long to feel her physical presence.

Lord, I miss her little hand in mine. I miss her thin lips puckered up against mine. I miss cutting her wavy hair, her fingernails, helping her button her pants, carrying her, putting make-up on her. I miss the feeling I'd get when she'd do or say something precious. My heart would literally feel different.

Lord, you were so merciful to spare Anna another surgery. It would have been terribly hard to wait for a heart transplant and then to go through all the stuff involved. My "mommy's heart" would have broken watching her deal with fear and pain. At least in this sorrow, I know she's okay and not only okay but healed and happier than she's ever been! She was a happy child. It's hard to imagine her any happier, but I know she is!

Lord, help me to always grieve with hope. I don't want to lose sight of eternity. I want to think of her and then think of what she might be doing in her bright, cheery, wonderful, eternal home! Help me to be able to move on in life as a joyful mother of children. I don't want to be sad. I just can't help it sometimes. There are times that I actually need to take time to be sad because if I don't it seeps out a little at a time and I feel like I'm always mourning, but if I do fall apart once in a while, I can get it out of my system for a spell. I'm so grateful my family has you to comfort and encourage us and give us peace and joy in the midst of this sorrowful trial. I love you, Lord.

A Fresh Perspective in My Pain

One day I was looking through Anna's school books, and I was sad that I wouldn't have the opportunity to continue to teach her from those books. She was such a good little reader and had such a zeal for learning. As I began to feel sorry for myself, God blessed me with a beautiful perspective. I began to grasp my most important role as a mother. I needed to be devoted to teaching my children about Jesus, above all. How many times had I put our Bible study aside to make sure that math or science got done? There is room for both, but on a particular day if one lesson must be set aside, it shouldn't be the lessons learned from the scriptures or through prayer.

I was so grateful that Anna loved Jesus. What if she hadn't loved him? My greatest calling, as a mother, is to lead my children to a loving Savior. Jesus Christ. Their spiritual condition should be of utmost importance to me.

That was the day I decided that my goal in teaching my children was to place more importance on God's word and to spend time in prayer together daily without exception. I wouldn't ever walk away from a question about God. I wouldn't ever turn my back on a child that needed forgiveness. I would work very hard to reflect Christ in my life so that my children would, above all, have the opportunity to know Jesus better. That would be my most important assignment as a mother.

Journal Entry:
December 6th, 2004

Today we are going to try to do a few normal things. Kyle is going to go to work this morning. I think he'll only go for a few hours. The children and I will do some school. I really fear carrying on, but I know the sooner I face it, the sooner it will be okay. So, we'll do our best.

Lord, when Anna left this earth, it was so clear that the most important thing was that she loved you. The most important thing she left behind was a reflection of you. Her love for you was apparent, and she glorified you by loving others as well. Oh, Lord, let me every day be reminded of that! I don't want life to ever be the same again! I'm changed now and want to be changed forever! I want to serve you by teaching our children to praise you with their voice, their hearts, their instruments, their creativity. I want to be there when others need help or encouragement. I want to faithfully pray for others. I want to share your loving kindness with the lost. I, most of all, want to declare to the world how you've worked in my life.

Lord Jesus, you are so mighty. Thank you for caring for your child, Anna. Thank you for caring for her mommy.

If Anna would have needed a major, painful heart surgery, but I knew, absolutely knew, that after she was recovered she'd be 100% better, I would have been willing to endure putting her through it. It would have hurt me to see her hurt, but I would have done it with that vision of the healing in the end being worth the temporary pain and suffering.

God knows the end and won't allow any pain in our lives that isn't part of some great victory! He has the victory planned, so he doesn't withhold that pain from us. He is faithful!

Romans 8:28, "And we know, that all things work together for good to them that love God. To them who are the called according to his purpose."

I took time to ponder some memories that I had of Anna. One thing that causes constant fear when you lose someone you love is the thought of possibly forgetting some things about them. I didn't want to forget anything! I carried around a little notebook, and when I thought of things, sweet memories of things Anna did or said, or funny little habits or physical traits, I would stop and write them down. In doing this, it provided me with a feeling of satisfaction. I wrote things like: *When Anna was four and five, she would nap on Sunday afternoon's with her daddy,* and *she loved to "camp out" with her brother and sisters on Friday night in the living room, but she'd always fall asleep just a few minutes after the movie started.* I couldn't forget these things someday if they were written down!

Journal Entry:
December 7th, 2004

Last night Kyle and I went out for a few hours. We actually had fun. (I hadn't wanted to leave the children.) While we were at dinner we talked about Anna. We talked about this trial and how God was working. It was very uplifting. We are so excited to watch God use this situation and use us. God is faithful to allow affliction in our lives to keep us close to him.

I have been thinking about Mary. She was blessed abundantly to be the mother of Jesus. To be able to raise Jesus and cuddle him, teach him to read, nurture and care for him. He must have been a loving, caring, fun child—being Jesus! Yet, she had to go through the heartbreak of watching Jesus suffer and die. God blessed her so much by giving her this precious son and giving her over thirty years with him, but surely God wasn't any less wonderful and loving in taking her son away from her. It was, of course, absolutely necessary for the redemption of man! She must have been at peace knowing of God's great plan!

Well, Anna isn't Jesus, but God's plan for her and our family is still certain. I was blessed to have Anna for over six years. Oh, how she blessed my life! I'm hurting, but I am at peace knowing that God had appointed November 19th, 2004, to be her day to go and live eternally with him! He has a day appointed for me too, but until that day comes, I'll go on serving Jesus and making my life meaningful. I'll love my husband and my children and be grateful for every day with each of them!

Psalm 37:18, "The LORD knoweth the days of the upright: and their inheritance shall be forever."

Spiritual Encouragement

Have you ever wondered how you are going to get through something and in the midst of your despair God gives you glimpses of spiritual understanding? This is what was happening to me. I would wake up expecting to suffer through another day and the first thing I would see was a gorgeous sunrise! The sunrise would be so magnificent that I would immediately praise God. Often, God would use a visual, as in the sunrise, but sometimes it would be an inner peace or a thought that would prompt me or give me a desire to open up the scriptures, and then the scriptures would always give me something wonderful to ponder.

Not every morning held that for me, as you will see in some of my journal entries, but there were enough of them that they carried me through the more difficult days.

Journal Entries
December 8th, 2004

The sunrise is beautiful this morning. Wow! Hot pink and purple! Then...orange and blue!

Lord, thank you for the hope that you put in my heart every day. It seems each day you give me a new thought, a new meditation. You are faithful! Your word brings me comfort and excitement. It gives me a desire to serve you and to please you. It gives me hope and joy! Thank you for giving me your word.

This book of the law shall not depart out of thy mouth. But thou shalt meditate therein day and night, that thou mayest observe to do all that is written therein: for then thou shalt make thy way prosperous and then thou shalt have good success. Have not I commanded thee? Be strong and of a good courage. Be not afraid, neither be thou dismayed: for the LORD thy God is with thee withersoever thou goest.

Joshua 1:8 &9:

Cecily and I are clinging together. She needs a buddy, and I need her. It really helps to snuggle her and spend time together. Silas and Jonas continue to be goofy and that helps us all. They just keep smiling!

I had a new thought today. I've been telling people that Anna loved this or that. I should be saying and thinking, "Anna loves me," or "Anna loves pretty things." Anna didn't stop loving me or anybody when she went to heaven, but rather, her love was perfected. Things that Anna liked on earth didn't necessarily go away either. Material possessions aren't important in heaven, but that doesn't mean that she doesn't still love flowers and other pretty things. God is the one that made Anna uniquely Anna. I'm certain she didn't become like someone else when she went to heaven. Her sin was just taken away. Hallelujah! Anna, I rejoice for you! Thank you Lord for giving Anna a beautiful and pleasurable eternal home with you, her Savior and Creator!

December 9th, 2004

I woke up missing Anna so much. I can't believe how much it hurts sometimes. I just want to hold her and talk to her. Her precious giggle, I can still hear. The day before she went to be with Jesus, I said that maybe we could go to the zoo that afternoon, and she got so excited. She yelled up the stairs and said, "Guys! Guys! Mommy said that maybe we can go to the zoo!" She was kind of running and had her hands in the air. I can see the whole scene in my mind. I want to see her again.

Lord, I'm not crying because I think what you did was wrong. I trust you and am so happy in my spirit that you have Anna. She'll never again have to enter into a doctor's office or a hospital. I'll never have to watch her hurt or have anxiety about a future surgery or even a heart transplant. I am thankful for that.

Thank you for sending Kyle just now to hug me while I sobbed and then encourage me with the hope that's in his heart this morning. We enjoyed another beautiful sunrise together. Silas sat up from sleep and said, "Daddy, look at the sky! It's orange!" Daddy said, "God did that for Mommy this morning." His little squeaky voice blessed my heart as well. He and Jonas are both in bed with me. They are precious. (Jonas was laughing in his sleep too.)

Luke 1:46&47: "My soul doth magnify the LORD. And my spirit hath rejoiced in God my Savior."

Staying Focused on Purpose

As the days went by, I was so very tempted to feel sorry for myself. If I had any opportunity to sulk, I wanted to. God kept reminding me that I needed to work at healing. It was not going to come automatically. When I was determined to give in and wallow in self-pity, I purposed to look for some way to escape it. It didn't come easy, but I knew the end of such feelings was only more grief and heartache. I wasn't always successful, but I tried to turn every pessimistic outlook into something constructive that I could learn from.

Journal Entry:
December 10th, 2004

This journal is quickly coming to an end—and even that makes me sad. It's so full of Anna—but that's okay, I'll put it up on the shelf when it's filled up and read it whenever I want to. In the meantime I'll write memories of her in my new journal. As life goes on, I'll write down precious events of my life, and I'll be joyful and exited to serve Jesus. It's my heart and my goal.

Last night I heard from (somebody very special to me). I received an email. This was the first time she's been in touch since Anna's memorial service. She said she's been too busy to get in touch. I understand busyness, but I hope now that I'll never let busyness take me away from reaching out and ministering to a loved one who's hurting. I told the Lord I would never be the same. I hope that it's true. I don't want to ignore the truly important things. It's so easy to get caught in a rut and just make it through a day of dishes, laundry, bathing, meals, and cleaning. I know that I am serving Christ as I serve my family in these ways, and they are necessary to maintain a peaceful household. However, it's so easy to get caught up in these tasks that there isn't time for serving others outside of our home. I want my children to learn to meet the emotional and physical needs of others as God puts situations in front of them. If we can stay caught up on our household duties, we will be free to do other things.

It's important that I take time to teach my children to know about Christ—to desire Christ—to love and serve others. I'm sure that through this trial the children are learning more about our Lord than they ever have. They are learning about love, faith, hope, and joy in the midst of a trial. God's character is being revealed a little more every day. They are pondering eternity. They are desiring purpose. Oh, what a blessed opportunity for all of us.

I look forward to you revealing your plans for us, Lord. As our hearts heal, you will help us to carry on joyfully.

A Powerful Lesson in a Little Thing

Journal Entry:
December 14, 2004

Last night the neatest little thing took place. The children were dying for me to wrap some Christmas presents, so I came up to my room to do that. The first thing I wrapped was Cecily's baby doll. I set it on the paper, estimated how much I would need, and then I cut the paper. When I was taping, I realized that the pattern on the paper (words that said "Silent Night, Holy Night") matched up exactly right. I had come upstairs heavy-hearted over not being able to wrap up anything for Anna. In this little incident, I felt the Lord was showing me something profound. I felt he was saying to me, "Lynnette, you probably would have had a hard time matching that paper up, even if you tried. You cut the paper and I worked out all the intricate details. That is like your life. You are walking, and I am working out all the details of your life. As you take the steps, I will continue to work my plan for you. The whole picture and final outcome are in my hands. Trust me."

I was so excited! I ran downstairs with the box, snapped a quick picture of the wrapping paper seam, shared my story with the family, and cried for a moment....then went up to wrap more presents. Lord, thank you for that marvelous lesson!

Many people, including myself, would usually not take time to notice a little thing like this, but you see I was constantly looking for the Lord, in everything! I needed him desperately, and I was enjoying the lessons he was teaching me in every little thing!

It's a blessing when God is working so regularly in your life. He desires us and wants us to be actively serving and learning from him. It's never him that turns away from us. It's too bad that it's so often the life and death situations that cause us to seek the Lord, but often we wait for those times to actively pursue a relationship with our Lord. I confess it takes more effort to seek him when everything in my life is easy, and that's a disappointing truth.

I'm grateful for memories of little miracles that God has done in my life. I'm glad I have recorded many of them in my journals. These memories help to revive me in my spiritually dry seasons.

Not only is Christ the King of Kings and Lord of Lords, but he has taken time to personalize my relationship with him by showing me "a token for good." I wonder how many things I've missed along the way because I was too busy to notice. It makes me think of the story of Mary and Martha. Jesus was in their presence. Mary sat and listened to Jesus as Martha worked to prepare a meal for him. She looked at it as service to her Lord, but she didn't realize that her service was the very thing taking her away from the one she served.

I'm guilty of this. It's an ongoing frustration, but God isn't done with me yet. I trust he will continue to draw me closer to him. I don't want any more painful trials, but my spirit desires Christ. He knows what I need and what will bring about good in my life.

Death and Heaven Provoke Thought in My Children

When the afflictions of life make their way to our path, we find ourselves looking for anything good that can come as a result of our sorrow. Somehow it eases the pain a little. One of the most precious results of Anna's death was the salvation of her big sister Cecily and her little brother Silas.

Journal Entry
December 15th, 2004

Yesterday was a day to talk about for years to come! Cecily Kate, sweet Cecily, answered Christ's call. She accepted Jesus' free gift of salvation!

She was helping me move some books to our new bookshelf in the library. I found Anna's little school notebook, so we began to talk about Anna.

We talked about her being in heaven. I had just shared with the children about something that Charles Spurgeon had said about seeing the gates of heaven opening up for a believer. Cecily said, "What that man said really encourages me." I said, "What, about heaven?" She said, "Yes." I said it was awesome that Anna was there. She then said, "I hope that I can go to heaven." It was the first time in her eight years that she'd questioned that. I immediately wondered if God was drawing her to himself. So, I took the opportunity to once again share the word of God with her, and it was that very day that she accepted Christ.

The rest of the day, that was all she could talk about! I took Abigail and Cecily to a Christmas tea at a friend's house and she told the whole party (as soon as we walked in the door) that she got saved! It was a blessed day!

Not only was Anna's death influential in the decision that Cecily made, but later in the year, Silas too acknowledged his need for Christ. He began to cry one day and said, "Mommy, I'm sad because I'll never see Anna again." I didn't want him to automatically assume that he would go to heaven, but he needed to know that Anna was there and that he could be too. We had talked about it many times before, but apparently he hadn't really grasped that truth. I took the opportunity to share the gospel message with him once again. "Silas, you can know that you will see Anna again. Mommy knows that I will." He asked me how. I explained to him that I had received Jesus as my personal Lord and Savior, so I had the promise of eternal life in heaven. I told him that he could be sure that he would see Anna again too. I then asked him if he loved Jesus. He said he did. We talked about how Jesus died on the cross as the final sacrifice for our sins. He said he knew that. I asked him if he wanted to accept Christ's free gift of salvation and become a Christian. He said he did want to be a Christian, then stopped and prayed to ask Jesus in to his life. That day he told everybody he had become a Christian, even the cashier at Home Depot. She casually said, "Oh, that's nice." It's likely she didn't have a clue what he was talking about.

I'm not sure Silas fully understood what I was telling him at the time, but I do know that he wasn't rejecting it and in fact was receiving it with all that he had. As he grows, I know that God will help him to fully understand this wonderful gift that he offers to mankind. I'm grateful that God is beginning to work in his young life, and I know that the heartache he has experienced from losing his big sis will continue to impact his life and his heart for the Lord.

Journal Entry
December 16th, 2004

(Like Silas) I feel afraid sometimes when I ponder the future without Anna. I hurt so badly, and I fear getting through the days to come. This scripture is convicting. "Where is your faith?" (Luke 8:25) If my faith is strong, I will still hurt, but I won't fear. I will know that God will see me through, and that he will care for me. He will be everything for me and everything to me. I have nothing to fear.

Heavenly-Minded and Earthly Good

One thing that can be a problem when we become too focused on heaven is that we can be of "no earthly good." I've heard statements of this kind before and never really completely understood them until now. I couldn't see how focusing on heaven could be wrong. I now see though that if we take our eyes off of our earthly duties as a result of our focus, we can slack in our God-given responsibilities.

The purpose of our earthly work is to glorify God with our lives. As we serve God, we will become closer to him, and others will see him in us. If our eyes and hearts are always searching elsewhere for God, and we are not seeing him in our daily walk on this earth, we cannot be accomplishing all that he has for us. If he has left us here, then there is still work to be done.

Turning our eyes upon Jesus doesn't always mean stopping what we are doing. We should apply our hearts to wisdom and see his purpose in everything we do. He has come that we "might have life," and have it "more abundantly" (John 10:10). My life may very well be one that God uses to draw somebody else to himself. If I'm not touching somebody else's life with mine, then perhaps I'm not serving God to the fullest. I want to deserve the words, "Well done, thou good and faithful servant." How can I be a servant if I'm only concerned about my departure into heaven?

I battled with this imbalance until my children brought it to my attention.

Journal Entry
December 18th, 2004

I have been talking a lot lately about how badly I want the Lord to return. I have been hearing things and seeing things that make me say things like, "Wow, wouldn't it be great if Christ came in that cloud right now!"

I didn't feel I had an unhealthy perspective, in fact, I think the Lord wants us to anticipate his return. He wants us to be watching. But, I felt so bad when Jared and Abigail said, "Mom, we are worried about you. We feel like you're never going to be the same. You just seem to have this strong desire to leave all the time." I cried and told them I was sorry. I don't know what it's like to be a child and go through something as sad as losing a little sister. I'm determined that they won't worry about me anymore! I need to continue to live and not have such a strong desire to leave. They are a wonderful reason to want to stay, and I want them to know that. I will be anticipating Christ's return in my heart and not so much outwardly (at least not with an unhealthy perspective)

A Time to Weep

Things were looking up. God was revealing more and more to me every day. I was feeling as though I would make it through this great trial that I was handed; then I found a note that warmed my heart and created a deep longing in my soul. The days following also held some difficult tasks. It was time to gather Anna's things and place them in the chest that we purchased for them. It was also time to start school back up without Anna. Life went on but without Anna. We would have to endure another season of mourning. It appeared they would come and go. As we got back into real life, the longing for Anna became great for all of us. It brought about some conversations that were painful but necessary.

Journal Entries
December 22nd, 2004

Last night I was searching through my purse for something, and I found a little note folded up. It said,

> Dear Mom
> All miss you
> Love, Anna

(Yes, it said "All for I'll")

Anna had drawn a picture of a house. It took me a while to remember when she gave it to me, but I remembered that she had given this to me the same week that she died. She was going to her friend's house with Cecily and Abigail, and she must have written that in the van. She carried a little notebook in her purse. What a special surprise. I said out loud, "I miss you too, sweetie." I do miss her so much and wonder how I'll ever go on with pure joy. I get little glimpses of it now and then, but it is so hard.

The thing that helps me most is my desire to give my remaining children a life that is full of hope, joy, and extreme happiness. I don't want them to grieve forever. In fact, I can't stand to watch them grieve now. It breaks my heart. I will get through this, and if my only motivation is for them right now, that's okay.

December 23rd, 2004

"Hear my prayer, O LORD, give ear to my supplications: in thy faithfulness answer me, and in thy righteousness. My spirit is overwhelmed within me; my heart within me is desolate. I remember the day of old; I meditate on all thy works; I muse on the work of thy hands. I stretch forth my hands unto thee: my soul thirsteth after thee, as a thirsty land. Hear me speedily, O LORD: my spirit faileth: hide not thy face from me, lest I be like unto them that go down into the pit. Cause me to hear thy lovingkindess in the morning: for in thee do I trust: cause me to know the way wherein I should walk; for I lift up my soul unto thee. Teach me to do thy will; for thou art my God: thy spirit is good; lead me into the land of uprightness. Quicken me, O LORD, for thy names sake: for thy righteousness sake bring my soul out of trouble....for I am thy servant."

Psalm 143

This is my prayer this morning Lord. It is my heart as well. It's not my enemies that overwhelm me, as in the Psalm, but it is my sorrow. This great affliction that you've permitted and in fact created in my life is a special opportunity to lean on you. You lovingly escorted Anna into heaven and will lovingly comfort her family. We feel this separation to the depths of our souls.

My desire is that you will carry us through this exceedingly sorrowful trial. Give us victory and thus be glorified! I want others to see you, to know that you are real, that you are loving and that you take care of your children. May our attitudes and our hearts be right before you.

Why do people cling to sorrow Lord? Why do people like to be sad and refuse to look at life from an eternal perspective? I don't understand, yet there are times I do it too. I wouldn't survive this trial if I refused to look up. My hope is in you, solely in you, Lord. You, your presence, your word; these things give me hope. Thank you for stirring my spirit and filling me with your spirit. May my life reflect love, joy, peace, longsuffering, gentleness, goodness, faith, meekness, temperance; teach me and use me. I am your willing handmaiden.

"Thou wilt keep him in perfect peace, whose mind is stayed on thee, because he trusteth in thee."

Isaiah 26:3

December 27th, 2004

Lord, I give this day to you and ask for your help in it. Give me victory today. If I look ahead, help me not to do it without Anna but with you and the assurance of eternal life in your presence. Help me to focus on serving you. Help me to stay focused on productivity, and let me stop to ponder your goodness and to share that with my children. As I make a new schedule this week, let me find plenty of spots for music, meditation, and reflection time in your word. I want to grow more every day in my love for you and in my faith. I want to be someone that people come to for help because my life reflects you that much! Give me purpose and let me trust you.

"Trust in the LORD forever; for in the LORD Jehovah is everlasting strength."

Isaiah 26:4

I needed to work up a new schedule for our days. I dreaded putting the school schedule together without Anna in it. So, I went ahead and kept Anna on the schedule. I pretended I was planning her day in heaven. Each time I put something in a time slot for the kids, I put something in Anna's spot, something like, "Story time with Jesus" or "Spend time in the garden with Samuel and Josiah." It was fun and was less painful than just taking her name off of the schedule.

Journal Entries
December 29th, 2004

I got Anna's precious belongings into the cedar chest. It made me miss her, of course. Her little shoes and bell bottoms...her bunny, Ilisha May, pictures she colored, her hair that I saved from her last haircut (and I'm so glad I did!) Someday these earthly possessions of hers won't matter to me because I'll have her again! But for now, I'm so glad to have her things to still have a little piece of her near me.

December 31st, 2004

Silas said this morning, "Is Anna in heaven?" I said, "Yes." He said, "I saw her last night." I asked him about it, and he said she was out in the church (a building on our homestead where we have had church services), jumping on the little trampoline, and he was looking at her. He said that Jared was being crazy and Anna was laughing at him. He said he was laughing too.

It blesses my heart to know that he was thinking of and dreaming about his big sister. It's difficult to know what it is like for the little people. I know that he doesn't fully understand what happened, but he's definitely noticed

Anna's absence. After he told me about his dream he got emotional as he talked more about Anna.

Journal Entry continued:

He then said, "Anna didn't go to that scary place, right?" I said, "No, she's in heaven because she loves Jesus." He said, "She's not in hell? Because that's the scary place and there are scary monsters." I said, "No, she's definitely in heaven."

Jared struggled as well, though not with the same things Silas did. He was more involved the morning Anna died. He was our only child that awoke that morning, besides Jonas, but of course Jonas was too little to be aware of what was going on.

Journal Entry
February 11ᵗʰ, 2005

This morning Jared shared with me, through teary eyes, how hard it is for him when he pictures Anna on our bed—dying. She was making strange noises and her body was arched and tense. This vision of her breaks his heart and makes him feel sorry for her. Of course I understand, because I struggle with the same visions, the same heartache.

I shared with him that he must take that thought captive and purposely set it aside. This experience for her was not what it was for us. For us, it was the final step of her earthly life with us, and our lives would go on here without her. It brought about extreme pain and sorrow, but for Anna, it was quite the opposite. It was the beginning of her life without sin! It was the beginning of her life with Christ! How can we feel sorry for her?

It breaks my heart ever so much to watch my children hurt. I don't want them to hurt. I can handle my own sorrow, but I can't handle theirs, they must. I only hope and pray that I am an encouragement to each of them. I pray I helped Jared today and eased his pain. I know there is no escape from this grief. We must walk straight through it and cope with it. In time we will make it through and will be victorious.

Yes, death does affect children more greatly than we can know. Silas wanted to make sure that his sister that he loved wasn't in a scary place. I'm not sure where he got the monster part, but that must be part of his vision of hell. I guess he's thinking of demons as the monsters. Children are so optimistic and hopeful that sometimes we think they're okay when they aren't. It's important to ask our children questions and talk to them about things so that they will feel free to open up to us. Scars may form if there isn't a way to release their pain and learn from their sorrow.

Searching for Victory

When a storm hits, the wind blows, the rain falls, and the thunder crashes; it's a frightening experience. You take precautions and do what you need to in order to survive the storm. After the storm, you crawl out of your hiding place, you emerge into the real world, and you stare at the mess that the storm made. You wonder how you will ever clean it all up and make your property look nice again. Do you start with the broken branches lying in the yard or fix the shattered windows? This is the stage of grief that we were in.

We began to consider what we had been through and where we were to go next.

The children began to discuss things more freely, hoping that they were strong enough to do so without breaking down. We often sat together just kind of reviewing where we had been and where we were now. We took time to be grateful for surviving the storm. We were glad to be alive.

The days began to grow a little easier. My longing

for Anna was still there, and still is today, but the daily struggle with sadness was departing, ever so slowly. There is no fast track to healing from a broken heart.

I continued to use my journal as a release, but I wasn't writing quite as much. My life began to hold some routine and some regular duties. The kids got back to their school work. I began to routinely do my dishes and laundry, cleaning and cooking without help from others.

My house suffered because I lost interest in decorating and organizing. By nature I love to decorate and make the house look pretty, and I like things organized, however it took all the energy I had just to keep the dishes done and the laundry somewhat caught up. Usually when I have company, I will light candles and put a bouquet of flowers on the table, something to add a welcoming feel, but I found myself not caring. It just didn't seem important. I wasn't yet back to myself.

Journal Entries
January 14th, 2005

Kyle's out of town overnight tonight. It's the first time since Anna died. I told him we'd be okay. I think we're all doing much better. Most of the time I can decide when I'm going to cry and when I'm not, but sometimes it catches me off guard.

The last couple of months before Anna died, I was really worried about her, and I could trouble my heart with worry and fear in an instant, or I could determine to be grateful for that day and leave it all in God's hands. That's kind of how it is now. It is always there in my heart, this void, but I can carry on and leave it alone for the time being, or I can stop what I'm doing and miss her.

Any time I decide to or unwillingly give into my grief, I force myself to picture her in heaven looking down on me saying, "Hi Mommy, I'll see you soon! You'll be here before you know it and then we'll be together forever!" That helps! I look forward to spending forever with my precious Lord, my husband, my children, my parents, my sisters, my friends. What a day of rejoicing that will be…when we all see Jesus, we'll sing and shout the victory!

January 18th, 2005

Lord, you are healing all of our broken hearts. I don't feel as lonely and, it doesn't hurt quite as bad. I praise you for that Lord! I know your word is true, but I must admit I couldn't imagine the pain ever easing. It was just so bad, but you are faithful to your word and you truly are beginning to heal us.

Lord, you've blessed us so much with special relationships. Even though there were eight of us, when Anna left, I still felt lonely for her. There is a special little spot in my heart just for her, just as there is a special spot for each family member and each friend. A part of me would feel lonely if any one of these special people went away.

January 26th, 2005

When getting into bed tonight, Silas said, "Mommy, you think about Anna okay?" I said, "Okay." Then he said, "I'm not going to die, right?" I told him he probably wasn't going to die "tonight." Then he said he didn't like the "bad place." Then he started crying and said, "It makes me sad that people go to hell." I told him that it is sad, but Jesus died for them too, and if they reject him they can't go to heaven because the only way to heaven is through Jesus. None of us deserves heaven, but Jesus died so we could go there. I said, "When we love Jesus, we can go to heaven." His thoughts are awfully deep for a three year old. I read a chapter out loud from the book *Heaven* tonight. The chapter discussed hell, so I imagine that's why his thoughts went that direction. I didn't think he was paying attention.

February 15th, 2005

Yesterday I was feeling sorry for myself, and I escaped to the pantry to talk to the Lord. I asked the Lord, "Why do you keep taking my children?

Why can't you allow me to love them and raise them?" As soon as I said it, the Lord revealed at least one reason why, "Because Lynnette, then you never would have had the opportunity to trust me. Your faith and love for me are a result of my working in your life through these sorrows. Lynnette, you have treasure in heaven, three precious children."

I wonder, perhaps God knew that I needed these burdens and losses to be who I am. Others that haven't had to endure this kind of sorrow may not have needed it like I did. God knows us all intimately, and for some reason he gave the whole Kraft family these particular burdens to bear. He chose these trials for us.

I'm grateful God made it so immediately clear to me in the pantry that day. When God begins to reveal the answers to the questions that are on your heart, a feeling of satisfaction begins to settle in. You begin to see the worth of your trial.

Words from Others Can Help...or Hurt

It really is a very difficult and awkward thing to try to comfort a hurting person, especially if you've never experienced their particular sort of pain. I know that I've said all the wrong things before to others who were hurting, but since I've experienced three painful losses, I've also encountered my share of less than helpful words.

After Anna died, I must confess, I got my feelings hurt a lot. I'm not normally an overly sensitive person, but when I was grieving deeply, I couldn't handle careless comments very well. As I think back at the comments made, I don't feel the same way about them now. I hesitate to even write about them, because I know that I was often receiving them wrongly, but I know that other grieving people do the same thing, so I will mention them because I think it's important to share this component of grief.

I was hurting so desperately that I didn't have the strength to understand the heart behind the comments or forgive the words that were carelessly chosen. Here is a journal entry that expresses what I'm saying. I was trying so hard to heal and was focused wholly on *my own* heart. You will likely understand it from my point of view, but you will also likely be able to see what I missed that day which was my friend's attempt to help me.

Journal Entry
February 21st, 2005

I received a call from (a friend) that was really difficult. We talked about a few different things, none related to Anna. Then while we were on the phone, at the tail end of our conversation, she asked how we were doing. She said something like, "Having five other children and being so busy probably helps a lot with your grief." I said sincerely, not rudely, "If I had ten children in the house, I would still be lonely for Anna."

Then she said she felt she needed to share something with me that she read after her sister had died. She said, "I found myself crying all the time. I don't know if you're still crying but—" I didn't hear any more for the moment. I had to wonder at these words. I couldn't believe she would think that I wasn't crying anymore. Anna only died three months ago. She lived in my house every day for over six years. When I recovered from that statement, she told me that it's okay to grieve, but there is a time to decide to stop and begin to live again.

She is one of the sweetest most sensitive people I know. I pray my heart won't develop bitterness over this because I know that she must have only meant those words for good—somehow. It wasn't the right thing to say to a grieving mommy!

Lord, let me remember all of the kindness that this friend has shown me in the past. Help me to let go of what she said. You know, above all, how hard I'm trying to be strong. I'm trying to go on with joy. You, Lord, have given me great hope in my sorrow. But saying that...

I don't feel like I'll ever quit missing Anna. She was and is my precious little girl. She brought so much joy to our family- to each one of us. I pray that the hurt that goes with the longing for her will go away. Sometimes it is just so great.

At the time, these comments, and many like them, were hurtful, but reflecting on them and hearing the perspective of a friend, I realized that any attempt at comfort was truly an outreach of love. If people didn't care, they wouldn't have even made effort to console or comfort me. I was so focused on coping with my pain that I didn't deal well with anything else. We should always assume the best in people, and I tried, but during my intense grief, I didn't have the energy to do that. I truly wish I could have. I wish I could have seen in my friend's comments that she was trying to help me. She was right in saying that keeping busy would be helpful. She was also right to encourage me to attempt to look ahead and not live too much in the past...with my heartache.

If I would have told her that keeping busy was helpful, it would have been okay, but since she said it to me first I felt that she was being insensitive. I'm not sure what I wanted her to say. I'm not sure that anything meant to make me feel better would have helped. I think that the only thing I could handle at that point was pity and compassion.

One of the most hurtful things of all was when we heard through a friend that one of the emergency workers who tried to help Anna said that he thought that they (the emergency crew) took it harder than we did. I have no idea what would make him think that. Our daughter died with no warning. We, her parents, who loved her with all of our being, were in complete shock the morning that Anna suddenly left us. There was no way they were feeling the utter and complete heartache that we were. I'm sure it was hard for them, trying to revive a lifeless six year old little girl. It would be traumatic for anybody, but his statement was unkind and so untrue! If he could have spent the next year with our family, he would have realized how very wrong he was. I'm sure he went home to his family and carried on as usual. It took us months to develop a new normal; a new routine without Anna—my daughter, Cecily's best friend, etc.

When Anna had been gone just four months, we began attending a new church. It was difficult because the people in this church never knew Anna. They were getting to know us without her. To family and friends, they knew us as a family of eight and they could see and feel the huge gaping hole in our family, but these people were introduced to the Kraft family as a family of seven. I felt like they didn't *really* know us.

One day a family came to visit the church. Many of the other families knew this family. I began to visit with Shannon. It turned out she was currently going to church with a very dear friend of mine and she had heard about Anna. When she asked how we liked the church, I told her it was nice, but I was having a hard time because nobody knew us here with Anna. She said, "Well, maybe that's a good thing." I looked at her with quizzical eyes. What could she mean by that? How could it be a good thing for people to not know Anna? I don't really remember my words back to her, but I do remember thinking that she just didn't understand.

She spent that church service writing me the sweetest apology note (on a napkin). She gave it to me after the service. She didn't try to justify what she said but rather told me that she couldn't think of any good reason for that statement to make any sense. She said she was just trying to comfort me in some way and didn't know what to say and that's what came out. I was touched by her confession and appreciated her tenderness. I learned something from her that day as well: never to be too proud to just come out and say, "I was wrong," but also, not to assume that comments made are necessarily from the heart, because often they're just the first thing that come out of a person's mouth, and they may regret it the moment they walk away, as was the case with Shannon.

One of the most interesting things I heard was made by an acquaintance that we saw at the grocery store. She told us how sorry she was to hear about Anna. She then went on to say how easy it must have been to want to keep Anna at arm's length and not fully love her for fear of losing her (since she had heart problems). Whoa, that really threw me! What could she have meant by that? I loved Anna with all my heart. Why would I ever keep her at arm's length and not love her fully? I certainly didn't and never would have even considered such a thing. She was my daughter. Did she forget that momentarily when she tried to comfort me with those words? Would she have ever not loved one of her children if they had been born with a physical problem?

Probably one of the most careless comments made was made to my mom. She didn't tell me for quite some time because she knew I was struggling with feelings of guilt over things I had no control over concerning Anna's death. My mom was telling our story about the morning Anna died to some ladies that were working at a store where she was shopping (picking up some things for me). These ladies knew me. One of the ladies asked my mom if she thought Anna would still be alive if I would have called 911 immediately upon realizing she was sick.

My mom told this lady that she better never ask *me* that question. Being my mom, she was naturally protective of me and my feelings, especially since she knew I struggled with all those "what ifs." The only reason she ever told me about this was because we were discussing how people often try to console but end up saying things that hurt. We acknowledged that most comments, even the ones that seem the most insensitive, are usually not meant to hurt. It greatly depends on the personality of the individual. Some people think they are being helpful by being frank, and others think they are being helpful by being very emotional.

Two incidents come to mind that would describe how someone that is too emotional can say some really unhelpful things. I'll never forget the words of a friend during visitation after our son Josiah died. While looking at Josiah in the little casket, he said, "If it would have been up to me, I would have healed him." How was that supposed to encourage us? This friend wears his heart on his sleeve and obviously said this to show us that he was sorry for us and was just trying to show compassion, but we almost laughed as we discussed how silly it really was, and I'm sure he regretted it when he went home that day.

Another incident was after Samuel died. We had somebody in the hospital room that came to visit us, and she cried and cried and just couldn't stop. We were determined to rejoice and keep an attitude of celebration and gratefulness, especially while he was still alive. We finally had to ask somebody to, "please take her away," because she was bringing such a gloomy spirit to the room. She was just being tender (I guess), but it went a little (okay, a lot) too far.

Even though I had already lost two children and had truly grieved the losses, I found my sorrow after Anna died to be much more intense. With my babies, I grieved over what I would miss. I grieved because I carried them and birthed them and would not have the opportunity to raise them. I wouldn't be able to nourish them with the milk that my body was ready to provide for them. But I had Anna for six years, and there were memories all around me. My arms had held her, my lips had kissed her, my eyes had seen her, my hands had served her, my heart had loved her over and over again for over six years. I felt the pain to the depths of my soul. It was unbearable at times, and I looked for someone to tell me I wasn't going to hurt like this forever. I sought comfort from people I knew had been down this road of losing a child. There weren't many. I pleaded with them to tell me that it wouldn't hurt like this forever. For some reason, they wouldn't give me those words I needed to hear. Instead I heard, "It's going to hurt a long time." I wondered if those words were said to express sympathy for the huge loss that we had experienced, but those words only discouraged me. I needed to know that the pain wouldn't last forever.

I now know that the pain does slowly begin to go away, no not completely, but it certainly does get a lot better with time. I wondered why those people didn't tell me what I wanted and needed to hear (and they had experienced firsthand). Perhaps they thought that it would feel better to hear them say that they knew I wouldn't recover quickly thus acknowledging my daughter's death as a huge loss.

But I feared the future without Anna, and I feared I would never have relief from the pain. The scriptures say, "Who comforteth us in all our tribulation, that we may be able to comfort them which are in any trouble, by the comfort wherewith we ourselves are comforted of God," (II Cor.1:4). We should be quick to encourage others any time we can.

The Bible says, "Thou hast turned for me my mourning into dancing: thou hast put off my sackcloth, and girded me with gladness;" (Psalm 30:11).

It took me a while to find them, but when I did, I believed those words. I decided I didn't need man's words of comfort. I really only needed God's words. They were right there for me, and I could read them and be uplifted by them *whenever* I wanted and needed them. I would believe them and cling to them. If I needed words of comfort from a person, God would bring someone to me.

Despite all the failed attempts at comfort, there were people that God did use to help me through my sorrow. I had one friend that did something very unique for me. She'd call me and ask me specific questions about what God was showing me or how God was working in my life. As I'd talk to Barb, I'd find myself being encouraged as I'd reflect on what God was indeed doing. I declared God's work in my life, and as a result, I encouraged myself! And it was all because of a friend's concern and interest.

I very much appreciated this and as I look back, I find myself extremely grateful that someone not only took the time to be kind and compassionate, but also took the time to stimulate conversation that made me aware of the lessons that God was teaching me and the comfort he was providing. I may not have taken time to notice or declare these works if she wouldn't have asked me, and I truly think that she was excited to hear what God was doing.

Not only was I learning and growing, but so was she. In fact, she would write things that I said in her notebook, and then she would quote me later when she was talking to me. I hadn't even written these things down. I only shared them as the Spirit of God led me. I was amazed but pleased that she considered my words worth recording. (I may have to ask her for a copy of them someday!)

Another person that comforted me in my tribulation was my husband. Kyle was hurting as much as anybody, but his self sacrificing love was a blessing to me. He allowed God, once again, to give him supernatural strength to help me and the children through the painful days. He did most of his grieving alone in his car. This is a true definition of a man. Sacrificing for those he loves.

Journal Entry
December 11th, 2005

Kyle truly is my dearest and closest friend and my love. I lean on him heavily, and he continues to be strong for me. There are times that he needs me and, I feel so inadequate to comfort him compared to what he is for me. But my words do encourage him, I can tell. Being alone with him and talking about God's desires for us and our children is exciting. We both have the same heart's desire. It is obvious how much he loves me just by the way he cares for and nurtures me. He serves me in ways only he could. Even the cup of coffee he brings to me in bed in the morning ministers to my heart, or hearing him come quickly up the stairs to make sure I'm awake beholding the beautiful sunrise.

I love living out here in the country. We've lived in this house six years, almost Anna's entire life. I never want to leave this place. There are so many sweet memories here. Memories of the children playing—Anna and Cecily, sweeping the front porch together. The memories are hard because I love to remember her doing these things, but then it hurts. It's so easy to picture Anna's body lying there without life and feel despair, but that's wrong! That body had only the function of providing a place for her beautiful soul to abide while here on earth. It was an adorable body, God's precious creation, but Anna's life was within that shell. I'm glad that someday we will get our glorified bodies because God did create them, and it is part of each of us, but for now I need to remember that everything that was life in Anna is still living, only with Jesus, in her beautiful eternal home. The same one I will graduate to one day. I have great anticipation of that glorious day!

Death is a very strange thing, inevitable and natural, yet strange. It touches every one of us and eventually will come to each one of us as well, but when death is right in front of us, it really is a difficult thing to grasp. None of us will ever respond correctly all the time, but it's good to learn through life's experiences.

Just being there for someone is important. I recall being hurt when I would realize that a good friend or family member hadn't been in contact for quite a while. I momentarily assumed I just wasn't important to them. It wasn't rational but hurting people don't think rationally. The truth is, I contacted people who I needed to talk to, so even if someone hadn't been in touch with me, it wasn't really bothering me, it just began to bother me when I realized it. I guess it's really just a "woe is me" feeling.

I have one friend who would just hug me and tell me she loved me. She would say, "Oh Lynnette, I'm so sorry you are hurting. I can only imagine how hard this is." She and her family were there by our sides the day of Anna's viewing/visitation. I kept expecting them to leave that day, but they didn't leave until we did, which was a whole day sacrifice. She also helped me get my house together when we were rearranging to add a memorial room. Sherlyn is the same friend that called our house the morning Anna died so that Jared would have somebody to talk to while we were at the hospital. I didn't find this out until later. She prayed with him and had him make a pot of coffee just to give him something to do. I couldn't be with Jared that morning, but she stepped in and met that need. That's the kind of love I hope to be able to give to my friends when they are in need.

Another friend constantly met physical needs and tried to help me in the everyday things. Renee was just there. She was missing Anna too. Her daughter was one of Anna's closest friends. Being with her brought me comfort. She just took me to run errands and picked up stuff from the grocery store for me. She let me talk about Anna, and that is something that *really* helped me. Some people would avoid the Anna subject, and I hated that! Anna pops up in conversations every single day in our household. She was here for over six years and will be here forever in our hearts and minds. The piano that her fingers touched so many times still sits in our dining room. The plates and cups that she used are still in our cabinets. The toys that she played with are being played with by her brothers, and the books that she read still stand on our bookshelves. Her memory is alive in this home in our stuff. She is forever in our hearts, and the flashbacks are forever in our minds.

Many times God gave me the ability to rejoice in my trial, especially when I was giving a report to a friend or acquaintance. As I would testify of how God was working and what he was teaching me, I would see their head shake and their eyes show a great deal of admiration as if to say, "Wow, I'm impressed." They might say, "You are taking this so well! You are so much stronger than I

am. I would just fall apart if one of my children died."
People must think they are giving a compliment by saying
something like that. It seems kind and innocent enough.
I'll explain why it may not be the best thing to say to a
person that is grieving.

Almost all of my crying takes place either alone or
with a loved one or very close friend. I don't just walk
around the store crying or go to church and cry the
whole time, (although the tears have occasionally come
at some unexpected times and locations). Grieving is a
very private, intimate matter.

So, when you run into somebody and begin to tell
them, with a smile on your face, what God is doing to
teach you and how he is holding you together, they assume
you are okay. They tell people you are doing remarkably
well! I'm sure it is said sincerely and with no harmful
intentions, but I'll admit when people have said this or
something like this to me, I wondered if they saw me as
cold-hearted. I felt like they were accusing me of being
insensitive, like I was getting over the hurt too quickly.

I think that people can't picture themselves in a painful
trial that they've never experienced, and just like I can't
imagine what it would be like to lose my husband, and
I can't imagine surviving that, they can't imagine losing
their child and surviving the trial. So, they assume they
would just fall apart.

There are two errors in this type of thinking. First of
all, when you are a Christian, God gives you the strength
to deal with the trial at hand. His grace is sufficient for
each and every trial that he allows. If you are not in the

trial, you don't have grace for it. Secondly, these people aren't seeing you in your intimate moments, when you are at home struggling to pull yourself out of bed and face the day. They don't see you when you are trying to get yourself to come out of the pantry or the bathroom to face your family without the sorrow that has momentarily overwhelmed you. They don't see the daily battle. No, I am not the least bit strong. It's God that is strong! It is none of my strength; it's the strength of Christ that is in me. The glory belongs to God alone.

I realize now that no person could give me everything I needed. There might be a sweet word of encouragement that truly lifted my heart for a moment or a warm hug or a listening ear that eased the pain for a while, but it was only a temporary comfort. I discovered that God was really the only one who could truly be *all* that I needed. I leaned on friends and family, and their love and support did get me out of some ruts, but my true help came from God. People can help us focus our eyes the right direction, but our hope and comfort come from God alone. He is the only one that knows the outcome of our trial and he is the only one truly capable of changing us.

I craved the hope and comfort that only God could offer. I needed intimate prayer time with him. I needed to receive comfort from the Word of God. I needed him. I needed my Savior, my Father…my only true hope.

Dreams

It's obvious that some of our dreams must be a result of things we are thinking, but many are not. They might be stimulated by our fears and insecurities, our hopes and ambitions, and sometimes just crazy things that we truly haven't thought about in years or at all! But, I often wonder if God gives us some of our dreams. I've heard Christians say to not pay heed to our dreams because we're not in our right (sober) mind during them. I used to agree with that counsel, however, I've dreamed enough things that have prompted me to act that I wonder if God does indeed use our still moments to attempt to communicate with us.

Regardless of whether they are for a purpose or not, there have been times that they have affected me greatly. Dreaming was a big part of my grieving and my healing. Sometimes my dreams frightened me, sometimes they brought me joy.

Journal Entry
December 3rd, 2004

This morning my heart is a bit heavier than it's been other mornings this week. It must be because I had a dream about Anna last night. I've dreamt about her nightly, but this one was upsetting because she wasn't feeling well, and I was trying to comfort her. In my dream I was worried she was going to die, and I was despairing. I desperately need to remember that she is in heaven with Jesus!

I find it very interesting that when I am fearful of losing someone or something, I dream that I'm losing my teeth. It might sound petty compared to other things, but while I'm dreaming it, it really is very traumatic. I had this dream after Samuel died, after Josiah died, and at other times in my life when I was worried, especially while I was pregnant. This is a dream that came once again about a month after Anna died. That same night, I had another dream that I wrote about in my journal.

Journal Entries:
December 21st, 2004

I dreamt that Anna walked into the room where I was. I grabbed her and picked her up and was crying. I said, "Oh, Anna! I love you! I've missed you!" I was holding her so tight. Then I said, "Can you stay with me?" She started to nod her head, but then she stopped, shook her head, and said, "No, Momma, but I'll see you again." Her countenance was sweet, and she was very happy to be in my arms. Her sweet words gave me comfort. I knew that she was sincere. When I woke up, I really felt I had seen her and talked with her. My heart aches for her.

God gave me a verse in my sleep. I was saying the whole verse correctly in my sleep over and over, but by the time I woke up, I had to look it up to get it just right. It was, "Thou wilt keep him in perfect peace whose mind is stayed on Thee, because he trusteth in Thee," (Isa. 26:3).

Thank you Lord, for that Word of encouragement…in my sleep.

December 25th, 2004

I had a terrible dream last night. I dreamed that Cecily was dying. She had been shot, and I was holding her in my arms. I was telling her it was okay because she was going to be with Jesus. She wasn't sad or scared. Then I told her that she was going to get to be with Anna again. She was so happy about that. I'm praising God it was just a dream!

January 18th, 2005

I had Anna back for a little while in a dream last night. It was wonderful to see her, if only in a dream. It's interesting because in my dream I knew that I had her back. It wasn't as though she'd never left. She was back and still had her heart problems. I was talking to her about putting her on some natural supplements that would help her heart. She looked great, not swollen or purple. She was tired, so Daddy was holding her. She looked back at me with a little smile and a tired face and said, "I still like my naps." I wish I could remember what else she said, but that one sentence is all I can remember.

Oh, how I long to touch her and talk to her. There truly is a void in my heart. It's kind of like I'm missing a piece of it, and I don't want it filled up with anything else. If Anna can't fill it, it will have to remain empty. But, I wish it would stop hurting so much.

January 20th, 2005

Today my heart feels sad. I dreamed about Anna last night. It makes me miss her, but I am glad that she visits me in my dreams. I'd rather see and hear and feel her there and then miss her than not think of or dream of her at all.

It's been two months now, but the longing in my heart is still so great. I shouldn't do this, but sometimes I wonder why God has required that I give back three of my children. It is so hard to give birth to a beautiful child and then not be able to nourish and love him. Then it's even harder to have a dear daughter for six years; to play with her, care for her, love her, laugh with her, tickle her, teach her, clothe her, feed and care for her every need, and then have to be without her. Oh, I'm glad for the six years I got to be with Anna. I wouldn't trade those years for anything! But not having her now, oh, it's so hard! The way I miss her is pitiful…the sorrow so great. The tears are flowing this morning. My precious daughter, I greatly anticipate the day I'll be with you again! You are so special, sweetie. Oh, how I miss you and love you, Anna.

January 30th, 2005

Oh my goodness, what a strange dream I just woke up from! I was with the children, although I'm not sure where Cecily and Jonas were. We were at Disneyland. I was taking the kids on Space Mountain, including Anna! All of the sudden I said, "Anna, this is too intense for you. I can't take you on this!" So I got off with her and got Silas off too.

Next thing I know, I'm getting back on with

the other kids, and it didn't dawn on me that I was leaving Anna and Silas by themselves! I stayed on the ride for a while, but then before it actually got to the scary stuff, I said, "I can't believe I left Silas and Anna alone!" Then I jumped off and ran to look for them.

I couldn't run. My feet were very heavy like there were weights attached to them. I was trying so hard to run. It was so far to get back to where I left them. I woke up before I found them. I was so upset that I decided I'd better create my own ending to the dream. So...I found them safe and sound. Anna was sitting on a nice piece of grass, and she was holding a sleeping Silas in her lap. She was very calm and hadn't missed us at all.

I've dreamed many more dreams since this one. In fact, here it is over a year later, and I still have dreams about Anna, but not as often, and when I do they are usually not sad dreams. Dreaming really has been part of my healing.

Possible Sightings of the Spirit Life

One day Abigail and I went shopping for some things to put in the memorial room we were doing for Anna. When we got inside the store, Abigail went one way, and I went the other. I had no idea what I was looking for, but I had asked the Lord to show me some pretty things to add to the room that would put a sweet feeling of Anna in it. I wrote about that day in my journal.

Journal Entry:
December 31ˢᵗ, 2004

Soon after entering the store, I noticed an older couple. I ran into them both several times in different places in the store. I never said anything to them, just noticed them. They were both about the same height. They were thin and pleasant-looking, nothing striking, just soft and plain. The man had gray hair, and the lady had soft brown hair that was straight and slightly curled under near her chin. She had little round eyes that seemed to be brown. She didn't have much if any makeup on.

I kept seeing them near me, almost as though they were following me. It wasn't normal how they kept looking at me. I was seeing them in the corner of my eye. When I was in the floral department looking at silk flowers, I looked at them and looked right into the lady's eyes. She was looking right back at me. I wanted to teasingly say, "Are you guys following me?" But something kept me from saying it. Instead I just said, "Hi." With a nice warm smile she looked at me with a sympathetic look and in a soft voice said, "Hello." I felt like she knew of my heartache. My heart instantly sought comfort from her. I noticed that this couple had nothing in their hands, no purse, no cart, no items from the store.

Considering they had been all over the store, this struck me as funny, especially later as I pondered it all. They seemed interested in me more than anything else. I wondered as I walked out if I was in the presence of angels. I hope the Lord will reveal to me one day whether or not those people, (or perhaps even angels in the form of man), were there to give me a moment of comfort.

It's hard to explain the feeling that came over me. It was as though I was being divinely comforted. I'll never forget it. It was as though I was in the presence of God.

I imagine God doing things like that for his children. He loves us, and it hurts him to watch us hurt. I had the feeling I was being watched over, cared for, and ministered to.

There were a few times when I felt Anna beside me when I wasn't dreaming. Sometimes when I was praying, I could see her face smiling down at me. There were times I would hear her voice. Often I would mistake Silas' voice for hers. He is the only Kraft child remaining with a high voice like Anna's. Jonas reminds us of Anna all the time. He is like a male version of her. However, there were times that I truly felt that she was there with me, and I wrote about one of those times in my journal.

Journal Entry:
February 4ᵗʰ, 2005

Last night I went to the Snicker Supper at church. It was a ladies' fellowship. When we were watching a funny video, I honestly felt Anna's presence. I could feel her back up next to me. If I wouldn't have been sitting in a room with fifteen ladies, I would have wrapped my arms around her and cuddled her. I even moved my purse out of the way with my foot to make room for her! It was a very sweet, comforting feeling that brought me joy. I've heard people talk about things like that, feeling the presence of a loved one that had died. I used to think they were crazy, but now I understand. In an unexplainable sort of way, Anna is here with me. I feel her, sense her, and almost see her at times. I talk to her and can hear her. I can't explain it, but I really do! When Anna first went to heaven, I was so scared I'd forget her voice, her touch, and the way she felt to me, but I see now that's impossible! I experience Anna each and every day. It still hurts, but not quite as bad.

It's possible that I created these things, perhaps out of habits (like having her back up into my lap), but believe me when I say I never planned any of those moments. They were instantaneous. They were wonderful! I look forward to the day when I can ask the Lord if Anna was with me during those times and if he allowed those moments to comfort me. There really isn't any evidence in scripture that it absolutely couldn't happen, so I suppose it is possible. It really doesn't matter though. If it was just me creating moments to have Anna with me, well, they did provide something that I needed at the time.

Anna's Precious Belongings

One dreaded task was beginning to consider what to do with Anna's stuff. Items floated around the house for quite some time. At first, I didn't want to move anything because I felt like she was still here, somewhere. A couple of items had to go, and it was difficult. Cecily and Anna shared a queen sized bed. Without Anna, we knew it would be a lonely place for Cecily, so we decided to give it away (to a stranger). When the family came to pick it up, I said to the lady, "Enjoy that bed. Two very sweet little girls shared it until one of them went away." The lady seemed to understand how hard it was to watch it go. I'm not sure why I had to tell her, but I did.

I also knew that I wanted to put her things away in a special place where I could go back to them and look at them and touch them. So we decided to buy a cedar chest to fill up with her stuff. We bought a big chest and decided to put it at the foot of our bed. I wanted it to be in a place where I, or another family member, could go and be alone. It just seemed like a nice, intimate spot.

I found Anna's things around the house for months. I still find things now and then over a year later. I'll never forget the time, a couple of months after Anna died, when I found one of her dirty socks! It was so cute, formed to the size and shape of her little foot. I just held onto it and smelled it (no, it didn't stink, but if it would have, it wouldn't have mattered!). I rubbed it in my hands and on my cheek, and eventually I placed it in her cedar chest... one little *loner* sock.

In the cedar chest I placed the outfit that she wore the day before she died (unwashed). I put in a few of her outfits that she wore most or liked best. I also put in her special toys and dolls, a few pairs of her shoes, her coloring pages, notes, and art projects. I put in anything that had special significance or would bring us joy to see it.

When Anna was five years old, she had long hair. She decided she wanted it short, so when I cut her hair, I bound it in a rubber band and kept it in a baggy. Now when I pull that out, I have a little piece of her to touch. She had such pretty, wavy brown hair. It is precious to me.

Every time I found something and I put it in the chest, I would have a little breakdown, but as time went on, it got easier. I'm so glad that we took the time to gather her things and put them in a safe place. It's not the same as having her here, of course, but at least I still have something to hold that she held.

Self Indulgence, a Consolation

Barb is the friend I spoke of before who stimulated some wonderful meditation by asking questions regarding God's working in my life. She wrote to me and said that she had been reading a book entitled *The Lives of the Three Mrs. Judson's*. It was first published in 1851 and is about an American missionary to Burma; Adoniram Judson. He was married three times and widowed twice. My friend said,

Excerpt from Barb's letter:

… There are several situations of losing a child (or spouse). There was one phrase that stuck out to me. The strong tendency to self-indulgence which always accompanies a heart-rending sorrow. Have you experienced that? I have thought of you over and over as I've been reading through this book…

I thought her question was interesting, and I began to wonder about it. I began by looking up the term "Self-Indulgence" just to make sure I understood the term correctly.

Indulge: Allow oneself to follow one's will; to yield to an inclination or desire.
(Random House Unabridged Dictionary)
Self-Indulgence: Excessive indulgence of one's own appetites and desires.
(The American Heritage® Dictionary of the English Language)

I suppose this could cover a wide range of things. You could indulge in food. In fact, our family had a rule to only drink pop (soda) on weekends, but after Anna died it became our comfort beverage. We really did over indulge in it.

You might indulge in shopping for clothes, shoes, food, or even cars. If you were an organizer, you could become obsessed with projects like organizing closets or cabinets, etc. You could indulge in skincare products, make up, exercise, sleep, you could indulge in anything!

Would I have the humility to admit that it really was true? Kyle and I had discussed this before. Months after Anna died, we realized that our finances were in terrible shape, and we wondered how they got that way. We hadn't purchased any major items. We weren't buying an abundance of any one thing. How did it happen? We began to realize that it wasn't any major purchases that were hurting us. It was the small things that added up.

We didn't really over indulge in one specific thing after Anna died, we just didn't allow ourselves to go without anything. I thought through it carefully and responded to her letter.

My response to Barb's letter:

We find that it is a truth…at least for us. It is not a good thing, but it is something that our family has experienced.

It's like you look for things to make you feel better…even though nothing really does, except reading and meditating on God's word and spending time in prayer to him. This has been the most difficult year for us financially, and we think it stems from not taking time to be responsible with our spending after Anna died.

We didn't really over indulge in material things, but we weren't careful to be frugal either. We just bought what we needed and didn't really care about the financial outcome. We didn't feel like we should have to go without, because we deserved to have what we needed or wanted. It sounds really pitiful writing about it now, but it is true. You just don't want to suffer in any other way! So, self indulgence is probably a perfect way to describe it, but once again, it doesn't work, thus there is an end to this self indulgence.

How many people would think to ask such a question? We were indeed suffering the consequences of self-indulgence. Things that brought us temporary joy ended up creating stress in our lives later, and that really was the last thing we needed on top of everything else.

I also thought back to another time of grief after Samuel died. During that period of grief, we bought a piano and two cars. We never realized it until we discussed it after receiving Barb's letter, but we could remember doing that after each loss.

I was happy to receive her letter because it made me stop and acknowledge something that I had never really even given a thought to. Even this missionary whom she wrote about who also loved God had experienced this side effect of sorrow. How many others have done the same thing? Our transparency and humility will often touch others' lives in a way that can minister to and bless them. Now that we could acknowledge self-indulgence as a common response to grief, we could pray for others who were grieving and perhaps help them avoid making the same mistake we had. Identifying this might also keep us from making the same mistake again. Then again, it may just be an inevitable part of grief.

Firsts

The dreaded firsts are tough, and there are more than I ever realized! I thought after the first year we'd be done with them, but somehow there was always a new one. I remember the first load of laundry I did after Anna died that didn't have any of her clothes in it. There was the first of every holiday. The first time we piled in the van without her. The first time we went to church without her. The first time we had a family gathering without her. The first family picture…the list just goes on and on. Over a year later, I was still facing a first. When I was preparing our income tax return on-line, I had to delete Anna's name off of the dependents list. I knew it was coming, but even that made me sad.

The hardest one for me was Anna's 7th birthday, her first birthday away from us. Well, actually, the birthday itself wasn't hard, it was the anticipation of the first birthday that was. For about two weeks before the day, I was depressed. I had it on my mind constantly and was afraid of facing it. I didn't think I'd make it through the day without breaking down.

Journal Entries:
July 11, 2005

I've been struggling lately with depression. I wake up a little sad in the mornings, and I find myself longing for heaven, possibly as an escape. I think it's because it is July and Anna's 7th birthday is coming up. I'm anticipating a difficult day. I just carry this emptiness inside. Once I'm up and busy, I know I'll be okay. It's the idle moments that are so difficult for me, but I know reflection is important too.

July 17th, 2005

Tonight Kyle let me talk. My hearts been so heavy, and I've been discouraged. Anna's birthday is in eight days, and I wish, for me, she was here to celebrate it. I have to really fight to be content and joyful and feel like I have purpose. It's just not like me. I feel oppressed. I must refuse to give in to it. I know as I lean on my Heavenly Father who loves me, I will be victorious. Life will hold purpose, and in fact, does already. God has done so much to teach me of his love and his peace. I know he will use me as I surrender to him, and that is what I'm trying to do.

July 25th, 2005

Today was Anna's 7th birthday, and it was a perfectly wonderful day! All glory be to God! I woke up with my boys. It was good that I didn't have time to be alone this morning to think. I know God planned that!

Kyle took the day off and we went to see a fun family movie. We all enjoyed it. Today is also Mom and Dad's anniversary. They came by this morning on their way out to celebrate and brought some cheerful roses. Then they came over on their way home and ate spaghetti with us and watched family videos. It was fun watching Anna on the videos. When I first saw her, I wasn't so sure it was a good idea, but in the end I was so glad we did that. She's so cute! I wonder if there was a celebration in heaven for her today. I felt her sit on my lap tonight. I put my arms around her and enjoyed the sweet moment. I may create those moments without realizing it, but I'm not going insane. I'm just missing Anna. I really do feel her presence sometimes. I'll make sure I ask God about that someday.

August 2nd, 2005

I've been more alive lately! The depression is gone! I praise God! Anna's birthday ended up being a blessing and I have felt better ever since.

The first vacation we took after Anna died was also bittersweet. We went to Branson, Missouri, which is the only place we've ever been on a family vacation, besides Disney World when Anna was given a trip by the Make-a-Wish Foundation. Although we've skipped a year here and there, we try to make the short trip every year.

Journal Entry
September 4th, 2005

We just got back from Branson on Friday evening. We had such a great time. We thought of Anna many times each day. Jonas continually reminds us of her. What a treat!

I'm very thankful to the Lord for allowing us to get away. It was a much needed escape from the daily routine! It was our first time to do this since Anna's death. My, how we all miss her! I am so excited for the reunion we will have and am so glad that I can know for certain it will happen!

We gained strength and courage each time we faced a first and claimed victory over it! We began to recover more quickly with each one. I praise God for his help on those special days when Anna wasn't with us.

The Bitter Cup of Death – Hope Prevails

Another letter I received from Barb asked me another question. She said that Adoniram Judson (missionary to Burma) compared grief to "drinking from a bitter cup," and wondered if I felt the same way. I spent some time mediating on that and responded with this letter.

My Response to Barb's letter:

Yes, it truly is a bitter cup! More bitter than I could have ever imagined. The pain was deeper and the sorrow more terrible than I could have comprehended. Refusing consolation had its place. There were moments that I wanted to grieve my loss and miss my daughter as deeply as I possibly could. Then there were times when I wished for an encouraging word.

I wanted God to give me great hope and joy. Man could not really give hope. Everything I ever needed was only offered by my Lord. Mere man cannot truly comfort. Hugs and "I love you's" are precious and needed. Scripture and kind words are a blessing. However, there is only temporary comfort in them. It's when I would personally seek my Heavenly Father and ponder his workings and look forward to my eternity with him that I could truly hope. It was a hope that would give me a desire to seek him more diligently. It was a hope that would give me true joy in my trial. The sorrow would come and go, but the hope never left me and this is what helped me to carry on.

It is certainly true that in the end (and we are still getting there), that the joy of our eternity settles in and makes heaven seem ever so dear. A bit of me is there in my children. I feel as though a part of me has already departed this earth and has entered into heaven with the Lord.

What does this do to my perspective? It is different than it once was. It is more heaven focused. I live, not only for today, as scripture encourages us to do, but also with a heavenly focus as scripture also encourages. How will what I'm doing today affect eternity?

I not only have a desire to please Jesus, but I also picture my children cheering me on from heaven…encouraging me to fight the good fight and finish the race. See, I'm still their mommy, and just like in our present lives, we desire to live a life that our children can look up to and learn from, I still desire that with Samuel, Josiah, and Anna (even though that's impossible because I'm on this sinful earth in my sinful state and they are sinless!).

Her letter came at a great time. It had been over a year since Anna's death, and I hadn't really taken the time to stop and reflect on where I was. I thoroughly enjoyed receiving and responding to it and praise the Lord for prompting her to send that letter.

Victory!

What do I consider a victory in heartache? Victory is when you can forge ahead with a feeling of excitement for the future, not just tolerating it or being okay with it, but truly anticipating great things. I began to realize that not only had God worked, but he would continue to do so.

Jared, Samuel, Abigail, Josiah, Cecily, Anna, Silas, Jonas, (and Harrison who was born after this book was completed), and all future children (Lord willing) will have taught us things about life and love that we never would have learned without them. We will use each and every event as an opportunity to learn more about walking with Christ and serving him.

I pray I will be faithful to continue to share my story and that it will deliver hope to those who need it. I also hope God will touch many lives with it and that I will never tire of telling of it. It makes it seem worth it all when I can share even bits and pieces of what God has done and hear that somebody's life was touched as a result of my testimony. I want the opportunity to share our story on a bigger scale. I want others to witness the mighty power of God! But I also hope that God will give more to me. More trials? Perhaps. But certainly more love, more hope, more faith, more joy, more compassion, and more of himself every day. I don't necessarily wish for more trials, but I've seen God close up during them, and I acknowledge that his greatest working in my life has been through them.

There was a point when my journal entries began to tell of regular daily occurrences and didn't involve so much emotion. I could tell I was healing because my mind was not always on my injured heart. I was beginning to desire routine, beauty, excitement, and new experiences. I no longer felt a desire to leave everything alone so I wouldn't forget what was. I craved some new things. I was writing in my journal about my little boys and the silly things we were doing. Notice the change of content in this journal entry.

Journal Entry
November 3rd, 2005

Silas is so cute! He's been doing Tigger, his little woo-hoo-hoo-hoo! Tonight after our Bible time, Silas prayed and said, "Please help nobody to get shot." I said, "Why do you pray for that?" He said, "Because, I don't want anybody to get shot!" Okaaay...

Jonas is crazy. He rides their bouncy horse like a maniac! I'm so afraid he's going to fly off of it! He wrestles with Silas and jumps off the couch like he's Superman. He's not always tough though, he's so sweet and adorable too. When we ask him what his name is, he says, "Jo Jo!"

He loves milk and calls it "noke." He's going through a Pooh Bear phase. He loves the videos. In his sleep the other night he was crying and he said, "Pooh Bear!"

Last night Cecily was in the bathroom singing her heart out. It was hilarious! We all went into the room next to the bathroom and stood there and listened to her. We were trying to laugh quietly, but it was so funny. When she came out, all six of us were there, so she jumped and said, "Whoa!"

"There is joy…joy…joy in serving Jesus, joy that throbs within my heart. Every moment, every hour, as I draw upon his power. There is joy, joy, joy that never shall depart." (Words and Music: Oswald J. Smith and Bentley D. Ackley)

You may think joy is gone, but it's not. The trials that we face in life give us opportunity to keep digging up that joy that the stresses of daily life tend to steal from us. When we truly know Jesus, it's in our souls and never leaves us. There were days I didn't think I felt joy at all, but what is joy anyway? I like the definition that says, "to take pleasure" or "to rejoice." (The American Heritage

Dictionary) Yes, we do rejoice and take pleasure when God is working in our life. Our flesh can feel sad while our Spirit continually rejoices! We know according to Matthew 26:41 that, "...the spirit is indeed willing, but the flesh is weak."

As I began to consider how I would end this book, I wondered how I would ever be able to put an end on paper to what was ongoing in my life. Do we ever stop learning and growing in our walk with Jesus? Does God ever take a break from teaching us and showing himself to us? No, God, our loving Creator is our Heavenly Daddy. He is always interested in helping us learn how to do things, how to respond correctly, how to have faith and courage, how to love others, and how to be victorious and pleasing to him in everything!

Do you remember when you first learned how to ride a bike? Your dad probably gave you instruction first and then added in a pep talk. After that, he held the bike while you pedaled. Then he began to run beside you while holding onto the back of your seat. Eventually, when he knew you were ready, he let go and you were off!

God is faithful to teach us one step at a time. He'll give us instruction then give us the pep talk. He'll walk with us and then run with us until he feels we are ready for whatever it is he has called us to do. Then he will let go...and let us fly! We will be able to accomplish each task that he has for us, because he will have equipped us for it. He'll start the whole process over each time he calls us to something new. There may be times when we fall off the bike, so to speak, but he'll always be there to put us back on and start all over again…instruction, pep talk, etc. God is continually teaching and we are continually learning.

As I began to flip back through my journal to see what else I wanted to glean from it for the ending of this book, I realized with great joy that God wrote the ending of my book before I did. On November 19th, 2005, the one year anniversary of Anna's death, God gave me words that looking back, even I was surprised by. There was resolve that I didn't even realize came to me that day. I hope that this journal entry will encourage you as much as it did me. May God bless you as you look to Jesus and let him turn your afflictions into triumphs!

Journal Entry
November 19th, 2005

It's been exactly one year today since Anna received the blessing of heaven and her eternity with her Savior, and we were left here to greatly suffer without her.

We all miss Anna so much and will until the day we are with her again. Sometimes it still hurts so much and other times we're okay. All in all, we're joyful in our spirit and greatly anticipate our future with Anna and with Samuel and Josiah and with Jesus.

Today I woke up a little heavy-hearted, and the reality of this being the anniversary of Anna's death came to me on and off all day, but we had a nice day as a family. Kyle had a wonderful parable for us this morning at breakfast. The message to us was that compared to what is in store for us (being heaven), life on this earth is not much, but we can serve Christ with great anticipation of our future. Anna and Samuel and Josiah have had their healing—we rejoice for them and await our own!

After being treated to lunch by some special friends, we went to the cemetery and took a fresh bouquet of cheery pink and purple flowers to Anna. (Her favorite colors.) She would have loved them. They'll be wilted tomorrow, but it doesn't matter, it was worth the joy it brought us today!

We put up our Christmas tree tonight in honor of Anna. It will be the day we put up the tree every year. I'll never forget Anna's eyes when we put up the tree last year. We put it up early, after conceding from much begging. She loved every bit of it! I wonder if she looked down from heaven tonight. Cecily and Silas were helping me by putting up bulbs. They kept saying, "Hi, Anna! Isn't it pretty?" Silas often says he wants her to come back and I always have to explain that next time we see her will be when we go to where she is. It's so hard for him to grasp.

My precious Lord, I don't know why you've chosen this painful path for my family. Anna's going away has caused the deepest sorrow any of us have ever felt. I've experienced your comfort though, Lord. I've experienced you in a way many never do. You've cared for me as a bird with a broken wing, carefully handling my injuries, preparing me for future flight.

My heart will never be the same. You've imprinted a love for Anna Gabrielle there and that lonely spot won't be satisfied until the day I hold her again. That's okay though, because as a result of that lonely spot, I've gained compassion for others and a strong desire to be in your holy presence here on earth and especially in heaven.

Anna serves you perfectly now, what an awesome blessing! I desire you with all my heart, yet there are days I don't heed to your holy call. It's frustrating, but even that makes me desire you. Everything I am and want to be is a result of your working in my life. I praise you for taking three of my children to be with you because a part of me has gone with them. I find myself holding much more loosely to this earthly place and the things in it. I can truly say I'm thankful for my sorrow because I've gained so much.

"I know, O LORD, that thy judgments are right and that thou, in faithfulness hast afflicted me," (Psalm 119:75). "Before I was afflicted I went astray, but now have I kept thy word."

Psalm 119:67

You are my all! May I remain faithful until the end and glorify you with all that I am, all that I have, and all that I'm given. Because of you, Jesus, I lift my voice and heart to you and bow before your throne with thanksgiving.

Amen.

Poems Written For Anna

A Special Heart
By Heather Pentimone

We're touched by this home-going
Of a precious little girl
Among God's many treasures,
A rare and special pearl.

The doctors warned her heart was small
Half the size of all the rest,
But they were wrong, her heart was huge,
To which we all attest.

Her joyful ways, her happy face,
Her love for those she met,
Could only be from a heart so full,
It looked to give and not to get.

Perhaps she couldn't run and jump
As much as others do,
But through her trials and times of pain
Her joy was always true.

The little heart is quiet now,
Her eyes are closed in rest,
But the joyful heart that loved her God
Lives on among the blest.

To My Dear Family
By Dan Pentimone

I know you weep and hurt inside
Whenever you think of me.
But please remember this today;
My pain is gone, you see.

My life was just a fleeting breath,
So quickly passed away.
Your love, your touch, your tenderness
Was always there to stay.

You sacrificed for me so oft,
You taught me from God's Word.
Because you cared, you loved, you prayed
Of Jesus I had heard.

Although you miss me now so much,
In His arms I safely rest.
How I wish I could comfort you,
But Jesus can do that best.

As you face each coming day,
I know you'll think of me.
Please look to Christ and think of Him
And trust in His mercy.

When you lie awake at night,
Do not be sad for me.
For I am sweetly comforted,
Through faith, I hope you'll see.

Until your life on earth is done,
Be faithful until then.
When God in his Enduring Love,
Allows us to meet again.

Through faith we understand: Hebrews 11:2

Afterword

Two years after this book was completed, while I was doing the final draft for publishing and Kyle and I were preparing to begin our ministry, Kyle contacted 911 *Dispatch* to see if we could get a copy of the call made the morning Anna died. We knew it would be extremely difficult to hear the tape, and we didn't know if we'd use it, but we thought it might be helpful in preparing a presentation for presenting our testimony.

We were extremely moved and elated when we received this letter from the 911 dispatcher. God showed us through this letter that he had worked in ways that we hadn't even realized. I find myself wondering how many more stories are out there like this one that we may never know about...until we get to heaven.

Mr. and Mrs. Kraft,

When Kyle called me this morning, I was unprepared for the rush of intense emotion that came to me. At the risk of being too forward, I would like to share a few thoughts with you. Though we don't know each other, ever since November 19th, 2004, your family has been in my thoughts and prayers. That early morning call in November has been with me ever since we hung up.

Through 911, I have been involved in countless tragedies, and I have interacted with people in all levels and causes of duress. Those experiences have taught me how to place such difficulties in a context and in a perspective that always causes me pain but do not cause me to be incapacitated with grief. However, that call literally devastated me for weeks after. I remember being tearful and easily overwhelmed. I questioned my work and whether I wanted to continue dispatching. I remember my wife not understanding my depression, and I remember breaking down at the dispatch console while reading Anna's obituary. I cut the obituary out and put it in my wallet. I still get tearful when I relate that experience to other dispatchers.

With time, faith, and support from my co-workers, I guess I somewhat came to grips with your tragedy. I have always wished there was more I could have done for her and more that I could have done for your family. My prayers were the best I could offer.

It's not often that we realize how people touch the lives of others. I just want you to know how much the passing of Anna and being with you during that painful time for your family has touched my life. In my wallet I still carry her obituary with the very sweet picture of her as a reminder and a commitment to always do the best I can in my career. And I believe that commitment in turn helps me to help others who are facing tragedy. So her life and death continue to impact the lives' of others in need in ways that only God knows.

Thank you for reading my thoughts and may God bless your family.

Courtney Becker